the Empty Pew

caring for those who leave

Louis Tamminga

FAITH ALIVE®
Christian Resources

Louis Tamminga is a retired minister in the Christian Reformed Church. For many years he was director of CRC Pastor-Church Relations Services. He has pastored churches in Iowa and in British Columbia, Alberta, and Ontario, Canada, and has served with CRC World Missions. Tamminga resides in Grand Rapids, Michigan.

Faith Alive Christian Resources published by CRC Publications.

We welcome your comments. Call us at 1-800-333-8300 or e-mail us at editors@faithaliveresources.org.

Library of Congress Cataloging-in-Publication Data

Tamminga, Louis J., 1930-

The empty pew: caring for God's wandering sheep / Louis Tamminga.

p. cm.

Includes bibliogrpahical references.

ISBN 1-56212-979-1 (alk. paper)

1. Church work with ex-church members. I. Title.

BV4013.T36 2004

253—dc22

2003027491

10 9 8 7 6 5 4 3 2 1

to Jean,
my companion in caring

Contents

Preface

This book is about helping churches in an urgent but difficult ministry. Reaching out to those who have turned their backs upon their church is never easy.

For many years, as a pastor and an elder, I have felt the pain of members leaving their church because, for some reason, they no longer valued their membership. I have sat down with many of them. I have pleaded with them. I have prayed with them, and I have prayed for them. Yet I have seen them go. Their absence left empty places. I have talked with their loved ones and shared their grief.

I have also pondered long and hard at what churches can do about the "back door." I have interviewed ministers, youth leaders, church members, and some of those who left.

On the following pages you'll find some observations, explanations, and advice that I pray will be of help to you in ministering to those who no longer join you in the pew.

I am grateful to all those who advised me, too many to mention. I have also profited from many printed sources, some of which are listed in the bibliography.

—Louis Tamminga
Grand Rapids, Michigan

Introduction
A New Challenge

Perhaps you consider yourself an average member of an average church. So it came as a surprise to you when you were nominated to be an elder and in short order were elected and installed. At your first council meeting, you were briefed and introduced to a number of responsibilities that would be yours for the next three years. At that first meeting, you were also given a list with names of the members of your district. Your career as a district elder had begun.

As the shock waves subsided, the one item uppermost on your mind was that membership list. You read it carefully. You recognized most of the names. You were able to match names with faces. But then you read it again, and you realized that you didn't recognize two names on the list. Did they sound vaguely familiar to you? Maybe, but you could not place them.

A few days later you phoned the elder who served the district before you did. You asked about the mysterious names. He hesitated a moment and then told you that the names had been on his list too. He had intended to contact them, but he had not been successful. In fact, he had postponed further efforts, mostly because he had been very busy and had not been able to locate the people.

You now find yourself doing a lot of thinking about the church. Somehow you begin to look at the congregation from a different perspective.

- You recognize that, though your church has known problems in the past, a mood of happiness and a sense of well-being prevail at present.

- The worship services are generally helpful, though at times you've wished members would be a bit more involved.
- The changes the council introduced gradually are generally for the better.
- Your minister has a pastoral heart and knows the Scriptures.
- The sermons are meaningful and address your spiritual needs.
- Your church has a well-appointed program. Every age group can find meaningful involvement.
- Relationships in your church are generally harmonious. Conflicts that surfaced in the past seem to be behind you now.
- Recently some of your members suffered illnesses and setbacks, and the outpouring of care and help on the part of the membership was heartening.
- Your church is definitely concerned about the new generation coming on the scene. Every once in a while a group of little children happily trudge toward the pulpit area, sit on the steps, and listen to an interesting object lesson.
- The overall extent of the educational system eludes you, but you feel fairly certain that the youth are well provided for socially and spiritually.

You now wish that you had participated a bit more actively in the church's program. You find yourself thinking again of the two names on your list. Do the other elders have similar names on their lists? One thought leads to another. You wonder if your church is growing. Well, yes, every now and then new members are introduced, young people make profession of faith, weddings take place, and infants are baptized. And isn't it a matter of course that churches regularly lose members? People move; people die; young people go off to college, marry, and settle somewhere else.

But then you think of the empty places in the worship services. Why would it be that some members attend less and less? What has become of them? And what about the others who transferred to other churches not far away? Did they no longer feel at home in your church? And you say to yourself, "We must talk about them at the next council meeting; we must do something about those who leave."

Your church is probably no better or worse than other Christian churches. They lose members, they feel bad about it, but they lack the resolve and perhaps the know-how to make this a high priority concern.

This book was written to help you and fellow caregivers in your church who desire to minister to those who left or whose ties with the congregation seem to be weakening, for whatever reason. Perhaps it may also help you and other church leaders strengthen ministry programs so that *all* members of your church may experience closer ties to their faith community.

Part One

Understanding Those Who Leave

In this first part, we'll look at what the numbers tell us about church membership and particularly what these numbers mean for the Christian Reformed Church. We'll summarize four main reasons why members leave and raise some questions to ponder in responding to those who leave.

Section One

The Importance of Numbers, Statistics, and Trends

What Became of Them?

Recently I visited a congregation I had served as pastor many years ago. What struck me was that many members whom I had known were no longer there.

That, of course, was to be expected. No one holds membership in a church forever. People die, and people move to other places. In several cases, the elders knew where these members had found a new church home. But in other instances, they were unable to tell me what had become of those who had left.

Church leaders and administrators know that keeping membership records is a daunting and time-consuming task. It can be frustrating too. Membership mutations can be complex, and members on the move don't always cooperate.

Take the hypothetical case of Mr. Abbot. He may have terminated his membership at First Presbyterian by joining Second Presbyterian not far away. Or he may have become an attendee at First Baptist one block away. Or he may have moved to another town where he took up membership in another Presbyterian church. Or he may have joined a church of another denomination there. Or he may not be attending a church at all. Mr. Abbot may or may not have informed First Presbyterian about his change in membership. First Presbyterian may or may not have been aware of Mr. Abbot's absence, and if it was, it may or may not have tried to contact him.

Aside from noting his name on a list, did anyone inquire about Mr. Abbot's reasons for leaving? Had he been happy at First Presbyterian? Had he struggled with needs or worries? What were his views and convictions?

Had Mr. Abbot been a participant in the programs at First? Had he been part of the leadership? What were the conditions in which he found himself when he left? Likely, no one at First Presbyterian knows.

Figures That Tell a Story

MEMBERS ON THE MOVE . . .
Local Christian Reformed churches must submit the names and addresses of members who move to a place where there is no Christian Reformed church to the Christian Reformed Home Missions Board (see *Church Order,* Article 41:5.a).

Christian Reformed Home Missions, USA
2850 Kalamazoo Ave. SE,
Grand Rapids, MI 49560
616-224-0772

Christian Reformed Home Missions, Canada
3475 Mainway,
P.O. Box 5070
Burlington, ON L7R 3Y8
800-730-3490

Good record keeping and a functional administrative system are expressions of pastoral concern. Christian Reformed synods have regularly urged the churches to make these prime concerns. Some of the overall membership statistics are published in the annual *Yearbook* (see Bibliography, p. 109).

Why this emphasis on numbers? To begin with, available records, kept over the years, will give us an idea of the extent of the problems we face. And that in turn will aid the ministry this book seeks to facilitate.

How has the Christian Reformed Church (CRC) fared in terms of membership gains and losses? Here are some trends and patterns that emerge from a careful reading of denominational statistical details.

In l963, the CRC counted a total of 256,015 members who found a home in 585 congregations. In 2003, that total was 278,798 members distributed over 995 congregations.

The composition of those memberships is more complex than it might appear at first glance. During those forty years, 92,446 transferred from other denominations into the CRC. But during that same period 163,627 CRC members transferred out to other Christian denominations. This constitutes, over that period, a loss of 71,181 members. While we're thankful that they found a spiritual home elsewhere, we must ask, "What were the reasons for so many to transfer out?" This too must be a concern for us.

From l963 to 2003, a total of 80,047 new members who had no previous church membership were welcomed into Christian Reformed churches. During those years some 69,157 members left the CRC without joining another church. The gain was 10,890. Some of those whose names were removed from the local membership rolls did not actually resign; they lost their membership via a process of church discipline (see Appendix: On Church Discipline, pp. 105-107), or their membership was "lapsed" (see "Synodical Advice . . .," p. 20).

The number whose memberships were terminated (69,157 from 1963-2003) has to be viewed in perspective. The average loss per year over that forty-year period was about 1,729. With an overall membership between 250,000 and 280,000, that number constitutes about 0.65 percent of the total membership. While that percentage probably compares favorably with other denominations, it's important to note that the actual resignations increased significantly as the years went by. In 1963, 375 memberships were terminated; in 1983, 1,777; in 2003, 3,011. The percentage has now climbed to over 1 percent annually. The trend is disturbing.

MEMBERSHIP RECORDS

"Each church shall keep a complete record of all births, deaths, baptisms, professions of faith, receptions and dismissals of members, and excommunications and other terminations of membership."

—*Church Order*, Article 68

The trend is even more disturbing when one looks at the statistics from a different angle. Forty years covers about two generations. Those two generations lost 69,157 members or about 34,500 per generation. This latter perspective more justly demonstrates the tragedy of this trend.

Church statisticians know that these figures are tentative. Individual churches may use different criteria in determining what constitutes resignations or terminations. The figures themselves may not be completely accurate. It is generally thought that the actual total of membership losses is higher than reported in the denomination's *Yearbook.* Some local churches may not have recorded every departure. Others may have sent transfer certificates of certain members to other churches, but the new churches may not have claimed them as members. Churches may even have lost track of those who've stopped attending without recording that reality and without providing ongoing pastoral care.

This lack of accurate numbers is part of the larger pattern. From interviews conducted, it appears that little is known about the 69,157 members who left without joining another church. What became of them? Did they join other churches? Did some of them actually become "unbelievers"? Do they harbor anger toward their previous churches? Did some of them return to a Christian Reformed church at a later date? Did they give their children a Christian upbringing? Faced with the reality that each year more than 20 percent of the populations of Canada and the United States move, churches will increasingly be challenged in tracking members who leave.

Another thing should be noted. Membership statistics show that the CRC as a denomination has grown only marginally these last forty years. During those years, 217,036 children were baptized while 62,292 members died. Internal growth alone should have increased the membership by 154,744. The actual increase was 22,798.

In the 1990s, congregations in all denominations started talking about the "front door" and the "back door." As new members came in through the front door, others left through the back door. The Christian Reformed Church is no exception.

THE CHRISTIAN REFORMED CHURCH

Membership Numbers

1963:	**256,015** members in **585** churches
2003:	**278,798** members in **995** churches

From 1963 to 2003

Baptisms:	217,036
Deaths:	62,292
Potential internal growth:	154,774
Actual growth from all sources:	22,798
Transferred in:	92,446
Transferred out:	163,627
Net loss:	71,181
Joined through evangelism:	80,047
Left without joining another church:	69,157
Net gain:	10,890

—*Yearbook 2003*, © 2003, Christian Reformed Church in North America

How Should Christian Reformed Churches Respond?

Evangelism must be a primary concern of the churches (Matt. 10:32, 33; 28:19, 20; 1 Pet. 3:15). But we must also be very concerned about people who have a foot out the back door. We must try to become churches of such quality that our members will want to stay with us. This holds not only for members who stop attending altogether but also for those who join other denominations. Where did the CRC fail them?

In their desire to keep membership records current, local churches have now and then embarked upon an action that some call "cleaning the membership rolls." Councils should always test their motives for this activity. It should never be an end in itself. Its aim should be to account for every member in order to minister to each one more effectively. Regularly upgrading and checking a membership list will assure the council that no one is missed in the pastoral care program of the church.

In ministering to those who do leave, we may use a three-pronged approach. We must ask,

- What do we know about those who became disaffected with the church?
- How can we best minister to them?
- How can we improve our present ministries and pastoral care programs in order to prevent membership disaffection in the future?

Points to Ponder

- Are you fairly certain that your congregation has a good administrative system? Do you know how it works? Ask the membership secretary to show and explain the membership records to you. ⇒ Don't have one
- Has your church council published figures on your local membership trends?
- Is your congregation growing? From what sources? Were there losses? As a council, have you considered what became of those who left?

OUT THE BACK DOOR

John Detterick, speaking for the Presbyterian Church (USA), a denomination that has lost two million members since 1961, says,

"We're not losing members to other churches; we're losing them out of the back door. They leave and don't go anywhere else."

—*The Banner*, June 2003

SYNODICAL ADVICE

"Members who move to localities where there is no Christian Reformed church may, upon their request, either retain their membership in the church of their former residence, or have their certificates sent to the nearest Christian Reformed church."

—*Church Order,* Article 67

The CRC synod of 1974 introduced the designation *lapsed membership.* Synod stated that "members who move away . . . may retain their membership in their home church at their request and with the consent of the consistory. If they fail to make such a request, . . . the consistory, having made serious attempts to rectify the situation, may declare their membership lapsed after two years."

—*Acts of Synod 1974,* pp. 81-82

The CRC synod of 1976 added another dimension to the lapsed membership procedure. Councils may declare a membership lapsed when a member fails to participate in the life of the church for a period of two years. The person must claim to still be committed to the Christian faith and worshiping elsewhere, and the council must not be aware of any public sin requiring discipline.

—*Acts of Synod 1976,* p. 25

The CRC synod of 1998 adopted the term *inactive members* for reporting purposes. It stated: "Inactive members are those . . . members who are declared by the consistory to have a relationship to the congregation which has ceased for one year." (The names placed on the list of inactive members are not counted by the churches in calculating their financial share toward denominational ministries.)

—*Agenda for Synod 1998,* p. 215; *Acts of Synod 1998,* p. 410

Section Two

Those Who Left: Who Are They and Why Did They?

Many Reasons, Many Roads

Even scant observation of membership trends reveals that those leaving their churches do so for widely different reasons. Here are some possible scenarios:

- Bert went off to college some distance from his home town. Studies and employment encroached on his Sundays, and in the course of time he gave up on regular church attendance.
- Maria, a young professional, met and married a young man who was not a Christian. After some time, she gave up on trying to fit a whole new set of realities into her church membership routine.
- From his teenage years on, William has been disappointed with Christian churches everywhere. He says that they are unaware of the sufferings of the world and uninterested in the issues of society.
- In their marriage, Joy was spiritually stronger than Jon. When she died of cancer, Jon and the children continued to go to church, but when the children left the house, Jon stopped going.
- Kate and Jack and their three young children moved to another part of the country where their denomination was not represented. They visited different churches but postponed joining one.
- Mary, a middle-aged widow, had found a great deal of fulfillment in the church choir. When a conflict erupted among the choir members, she attended church less frequently. She visited other churches occasionally but now most Sundays watches a church service on TV.
- After Tom and Rose went through a divorce, he no longer felt at home in the church where they were married. Tom told friends that he had put his membership on hold.

- Jamel remembers attending church during his youth with some fondness. But his parents' divorce somehow ended it all.
- Several years ago Bob's pastor approached him about making profession of faith. Bob answered that he would want to be totally sure that he would keep such a serious commitment. Bob has not yet come to that moment of certainty.
- Neil and Sharon decided to take their children out of Christian school for financial reasons. After making this decision, they left for another denomination because they felt less accepted in their church.
- Peter, a high school teacher, felt uncomfortable with the new pastor's sermons. He and the pastor had several long discussions, but gradually Peter distanced himself from the church.
- Ernie and some school friends regularly played the slot machines. He ran up considerable debts. His parents pleaded with him to give up the habit. In the course of time, Ernie stopped going to church.
- Grace befriended a woman at work who had become a devout follower of a New Age fellowship. She invited Grace to accompany her. Grace was impressed with the helpfulness of her new friends and eventually joined the fellowship.

Yes, people leave the church for many reasons and exit in many different directions. Understanding why they leave can help a church strengthen its ministry and slow the loss through the back door, while at the same time opening the front door wider.

Four Basic Reasons

Dr. Ian McIntosh, in research conducted at Austin Presbyterian Seminary, Austin, Texas, outlined four basic reasons why members leave their churches (see Bibliography, p. 109). His helpful insights are summarized here.

THOSE WHO LEAVE FOR INTERNAL REASONS

The people who leave for internal reasons have failed to come to terms with the Christian faith. This may take different forms. Some drop out of church because they

- question the very existence of God.
- come to the conclusion that, even if God exists, he cannot be known.
- say that they have been unable to come to a genuine relationship with the Lord even though they have tried and struggled hard. Problems may exist in other areas.

- maintain that God does not require the sacrificial death of his Son to be reconciled to people.
- doubt the need for an instituted church and hold that God can be experienced and worshiped in nature.
- believe that human goodness is all that God requires of people; they do the best they can.
- know, in their heart of hearts, that the God of the Bible is real, but they find the cost of serving him too high and so they don't surrender to the Lord.
- never get around to making up their minds. (The story of King Agrippa in Acts 26:27 illustrates that this reason has hindered church membership for centuries.)

THOSE WHO LEAVE FOR EXTERNAL REASONS

The people who leave for external reasons are those for whom church life loses its importance. This may take root in two areas of their lives—within their circle of friends and in the activities they pursue.

Perhaps someone increasingly moves in circles of people who are not connected with a Christian church. He or she forms friendships in which the fear of God is not very much present. In such associations, church members usually keep their convictions under wraps. They adapt their values to a secular lifestyle, then church attendance slackens, and finally faith erodes. When repentance does not occur, such members will eventually stop attending altogether.

A similar process unfolds when church members become involved in activities not conducive to Christian living, often leading to a hedonistic (from the Greek *hedone,* meaning "pleasure") lifestyle. They may attend church less than usual because they spend the Lord's Day seeking enjoyment elsewhere. A variation on this theme takes place when a person engages in reprehensible conduct that becomes addictive, eventually causing the member to leave the church, or the church to excommunicate him or her from its community.

THOSE WHO LEAVE FOR INSTITUTIONAL REASONS

Those who leave for institutional reasons have difficulties with the programs or the governance of their church. Church members have certain expectations of their church. Where the church fails to meet those expectations, problems arise.

Some feel at home in a traditional worship service. Others prefer a more contemporary style. Some like traditional songs; others go for praise choruses. In the church's educational ministry, some prefer straight Bible studies; others like topics of general interest. Some like small group sessions; others feel at home in a classroom setting. Sometimes members are offended by practices for no reason other than taste.

Members are also affected by the way church life is arranged and governed. In this respect too, members don't all feel alike. Some favor a democratic approach in which decisions are made by consensus; others insist that the council must rule.

Most church members are patient and tolerant and take disagreeable elements in stride. But for some, their discontent grows, and at a certain point they feel that there may be a church somewhere else that is more congenial to their tastes and needs. They begin to visit neighboring churches, and one day they take the big step—they transfer out. And some—after visiting here and there—stop going altogether.

THOSE WHO LEAVE FOR INTERPERSONAL REASONS

Human relationships are mysterious, complex, and often frail. Good relationships are a foretaste of heaven. But when relationships go bad, heaven come to the rescue! Church communities are not exempt from conflict. It happens to the best. And it happens at the most unexpected and inopportune times.

When conflicts are not addressed and resolved at a fairly early stage, they may wreak havoc in a church community. Battle lines become drawn out and increasingly confusing. Anger grows. More people are drawn into the conflict. The atmosphere of church life becomes poisoned. Membership losses occur at every stage of the conflict. Many of those involved will leave, and the exodus will continue unless reconciliation can bring the factions together.

Sometimes conflicts arise because members disagree with the leadership, its policies, or its actions. The pastor, because of his or her prominent role in the church, sometimes becomes the target of members' discontent. When they feel that their protests have not been sufficiently heard, they may try to recruit supporters from the congregation. In some instances an accord can be reached, but in others, resignations may come in the wake of the subsequent skirmishes.

Some Comparisons

We may wonder how the four groups mentioned in the previous section compare in size. Which of the four reasons is the most significant factor in membership loss?

Researchers have found that those leaving for institutional reasons (those who become disenchanted with the overall ministry program of the church) constitute the biggest segment of the four. Findings vary, but the number ranges from 30 to 40 percent of all who leave (see McIntosh, Bibliography, p. 109).

This means that the quality of church life itself is a big factor in members' sense of well-being. Though the members may not always express it, most of them intuitively look for a well-appointed church program. The leadership of a church has a great responsibility. To "be church" is a serious business. The ministry of officebearers and staff has immense consequences in the lives of the members. Leaders should be observant about what goes on in the church, what the needs of the members are, and whether each ministry is well conducted. Ministries and program items that become superfluous should be discontinued. Needs and challenges should be addressed as they arise. (We'll talk more about this in sections 13 and 14.)

In our ministry to those who leave the church, we are hard pressed to avoid evaluating the situation, but we must not judge people. Church leaders must realize that the last two decades have brought many changes in church life. Individual members respond differently to them and also struggle with constant changes in their private lives. Those who desire to leave must not be seen as opponents. Ministers used to be called "curates": they cared for souls, they brought healing to those with needs of all sorts. We must also come in Christ's priestly compassion, bringing light, being "pontiffs," bridgebuilders.

Members who leave for interpersonal reasons (those with troubled relationships within the church community) constitute the smallest of the four groups. They make up about 10 to 15 percent of the total. However, broken relationships within a church have far more negative implications than the number of members leaving. Congregational health is adversely affected by conflict. The mood is soured. Fear stalks the membership. Suspicions are always just below the surface. Spiritual growth becomes minimal. The congregation looks to the leadership for protection from each other.

Members who leave for internal reasons (those struggling with faith problems) and for external reasons (those adopting a worldly lifestyle) each make up about one-fourth of those who resign. In our postmodern culture, it's likely that these groups may grow.

Some Conclusions

Researchers have found that about one-third of the disaffected members were generally not very active in the churches they once attended. But half of those who left attended fairly regularly and participated in the activities of the church. For about half of these members, the decision to leave was the outcome of a gradual process. That group testified to some soul searching before they made the decision. Only about one in five reported that the leave was sudden, mostly as a result of anger.

> "A member who for one year willfully does not participate in the ordinances of his church nor otherwise express a serious interest in the church, may be transferred by the Session to the inactive roll."
>
> —*The Presbyterian Book of Church Order*, revised edition, p. 29

Researchers also found that when consistent pastoral care was provided within two months of leaving, the chances of restoring members to the congregation were far better than when such care had been postponed. Church leaders need to be aware of their members' status.

Those who leave their church are often themselves confused as to what their status in the church actually is. Some 20 percent of those who left thought that they were still on the rolls of the church. This may well point to two wider problems, referred to earlier:

- the lack of uniformity among evangelical and mainline churches as to what constitutes membership and how it is terminated.
- weaknesses in churches' administrative systems.

Another factor is that some churches practice discipline, while others don't. Discipline procedures and practices themselves vary.

In further research, those who left their churches and became "unchurched" reported that they still prayed once a week or more often. Half of those interviewed said that they believed in an afterlife. And a slightly lower proportion believed that Jesus is the Son of God. About one-third of those interviewed mentioned that they may return to a church some time in the future. Those who actually do are fewer.

These observations seem to establish that outreach to those who leave the church holds promise. Much depends on the blessings of the Holy Spirit and on prayerful, thoughtful, and consistent care. We'll offer guidelines for how to reach out in the next several sections.

Points to Ponder

- Is it your impression as an elder or caregiver that your council has a fairly clear idea of what your members are like, how they live, what their needs are, what their jobs are, how they feel about the church, and so on? Do you know the members of your district well? Could you recite their names? Their children's names?
- Over the last forty years, the Christian Reformed Church as a denomination has grown only marginally. What do you think are the reasons? What could we do about it?

DEMAS: THE COST OF DISCIPLESHIP

"Do your best to come to me quickly, for Demas, because he loved this world, has deserted me and has gone to Thessalonica."

—2 Timothy 4:10

Demas is Paul's colleague in the ministry in Rome. Paul calls him "my fellow worker." Demas weighs his options: stay with Paul and the church in Rome with persecution a real possibility, or go back to his home town, Thessalonica, a much friendlier place. Demas chooses Thessalonica.

Paul calls a spade a spade. He writes a letter to his friend Timothy and tells him that Demas has deserted him. He also states the reason: Demas left "because he loved this world." The cost of discipleship is just too much for Demas. In the moment of crisis, he leaves.

Demas's absence gives Paul a feeling of forsakenness. In his letter, he pleads with Timothy to do his best to visit him soon.

Those who leave the church leave a painful void.

Part Two
Reaching Out to Those Who Left

In this second part, we will explore ways of ministering to those whose empty places we mourn. We'll begin with an overall plan for ministry and then give specific ideas for making a get-acquainted visit and follow-up visits. We'll also look at specific ways to reach each of the four groups of people, each with a different reason for leaving the church, we discussed in section two.

Section Three

Preparing for a Challenging Ministry

Catching the Vision

Ministry to those who have left your church must begin with a vision. Without a vision for those in spiritual need, a church will not likely succeed in its efforts. Usually this vision is developed by the spiritual leaders of a church—its elders, pastors, staff, and other caregivers—and has a dual focus: those who leave to join another church and those who leave without joining another church.

FOR THOSE WHO LEAVE TO JOIN ANOTHER CHURCH

Church members who become discontent may complain to other members, stop attending, and perhaps "shop around" at other churches. At a certain point, they may resign from your church in order to join one that seems more promising to them. Church leaders must honestly ask themselves whether they were aware of this development and assess the validity of the dissatisfaction such members may have. Questions might include the following:

- Are there weaknesses in the ministry program or in our own performance?
- Are we ready to discuss this with the person who sought transfer?
- Are we prepared to make corrections if needed?
- Are we ready to review the program and care practices even if that would be an uncomfortable exercise?

And apart from seeking to answers these questions, it's urgent that someone be assigned to confer with discontented members to discuss possible misgivings amicably. Early interest in the well-being of such members can prevent disappointments down the road. And where parting of ways seems unavoidable, it's essential to bid this member a gracious leave.

FOR THOSE WHO DROP OUT

Some members who leave have no intention of joining another church, or they are ambivalent about it. The consistory must do all within its power to minister effectively to these brothers and sisters. Leadership must strive to answer these questions:

- Has our church failed the members in any way?
- Does our consistory understand the needs of these people, even if it disagrees with their motives or convictions?
- Are consistory members given to argumentation rather than compassionate ministry?

FOR ONE

"What do you think? If a man owns a hundred sheep and one of them wanders away, will he not leave the ninety-nine on the hills and go to look for the one that wandered off? In the same way your Father in heaven is not willing that any of these little ones should be lost."

—Matthew 18:12-14

Leaders must put on the mind of Christ, who leaves the ninety-nine to go after the one who wanders off. To have the heart of a shepherd (Acts 20:28; 1 Pet. 5:2), leaders and caregivers must be concerned for the well-being of the members; when members leave, they anguish over them. Only from such a vision can spring the spiritual resolve that your church needs to sustain ministry to marginal members. Commitment is the key to successful ministry.

Vision must be translated into resolve, which leads to action. The body of elders and pastors and designated staff people must be aware of the need for ministry to the disaffected and must pledge their readiness to give this ministry an honorable and pertinent place on their ministry agenda. Many of those who leave the church have known trouble and sadness; they need to see Jesus in their fellow Christians—in you (Ps. 34:18; Matt. 11:28, 29).

Perhaps you are just one elder who is gripped by this vision. Do not hesitate to contact your fellow elders and pastors. Share the vision with them. How can your church give priority to those "wandering sheep"? Struggle with the questions, and then pray about it.

Lord, enlarge our hearts for those who have left us.
We grieve over the empty pews.
Use us to find them, to reach them,
to bring them back to the fold. Amen.

Getting the Facts

Your vision for ministry must be based on accurate facts. This begins with a careful check of the membership list. Every name on the membership rolls must be accounted for, including teenage members. Search your memories for names and faces that produce questions of where they are spiritually. A small task force, appointed by the council, can ensure a thorough and comprehensive review.

ABOUT TRANSFERS
Although we're often primarily concerned about members who leave without joining another church, be aware of hidden facts. For instance, a member may have left for another denomination, but

- has the local church of that denomination actually received this new member?
- is this member attending there regularly now?

Membership transfer documents used by Christian Reformed churches contain a return slip acknowledging receipt. If the slip has not been returned, the clerk of council should be alerted to make further inquiry.

Be careful of neglecting those who transfer to other churches. It's important that someone in leadership have a discussion with that member about his or her reason for choosing another church or denomination. Maybe it's not too late for the consistory to make amends or corrections.

And pay special attention to young people who have left for college, a job elsewhere, or for military service. When appropriate, your council must ask,

- Have membership papers been transferred?
- If not, have the nearest churches been notified that these members are in the area and in need of pastoral care?

Using the Facts

Perhaps your review will reveal names of some current members who attend less than regularly. Are they in need of pastoral care? An ounce of prevention. . . .

From all these explorations will emerge a master list of members about whom there is uncertainty. This list can then be placed in the hands of the elders who will provide follow-up work, contacting the persons involved and offering pastoral care when possible. (See the following sections for advice about making such visits.)

Only when the consistory has reasonable certainty that this type of research has been done thoroughly can it formulate and implement a ministry plan. It is then that numbers convert to people with faces and souls.

Points to Ponder

- In Matthew 24:10, Jesus speaks of the end times and says that many will turn away from the faith. Do you think that the membership losses of your church are an indication that the last days will soon be here? Why or why not?
- Have you as council members kept records of membership mutations in such a way that you are fairly clear what percentage of those who left moved to other Christian Reformed churches? To other denominations? Or failed to join any church at all? How has your current record-keeping practice helped or hindered ministry to those who have left? What improvements can be made?

Section Four

Formulating a Ministry Plan

Assigning Tasks

The time is now ready for a special meeting of the elders and other caregivers with the task force assigned to gather the facts. (If your church council has both administrative and shepherding elders, this meeting should be with the shepherding elders.) It's time to formulate a strategic ministry plan to reach those who have left your church.

The elders and the task force members should consider the names on the master list and briefly discuss the facts gathered.

The elders must then decide to whom the task at hand can best be assigned. One way would be to set aside two elders exclusively for the task of bringing appropriate ministry to the members on the list. If it's difficult for your council to free two elders for this challenge, the names can be divided among the entire body of shepherding elders. Or perhaps some wise and willing members in the congregation who once served as elders may be recruited and deputized for this task. Each elder should be responsible for no more than two or three names or households.

Making a Commitment

It is important that the elders discuss how to approach the task. A mindset of pastoral compassion and concern must prevail. Behind each of the names on your list is a person in need of spiritual healing, a person who may struggle with problems, needs, temptations, perhaps even burdens and pain. Your agenda is not to administratively "remove dead wood" from the rolls but to see where you can bring care and healing. You are a bridge builder between Christ and his church, the communicator of grace. Your sole motive must be to bring precious people to redemption or to deepen their spiritual well-being.

Some consistency in approach is important. We'll discuss making the initial visit and follow-up visits further in the following sections, but pastoral care training may also be beneficial for your shepherding elders.

Give this ministry some prominence in your elders' meetings. Allow time for reporting by those designated to carry out the task. While respecting confidentiality, it's important that the entire council be informed about progress and possible disappointments. And those on the front line in this effort must feel themselves backed by devout intercessors.

Resolve together not to postpone this ministry. Ministry postponed is often ministry denied. Drift is deadly. Procrastination probably contributed to the length of your list of those who left in the first place.

Making the Initial Contact

Perhaps you are the district elder who now wonders how to make that first contact that hopefully will lead to a first visit. You may find it a bit daunting. Ponder on it. Pray about it. Rehearse every bit of information that the task force has been able to find regarding the person you are about to contact.

A personal phone contact is a good way to go. After you introduce yourself and identify your church, ask whether you may stop by to say hello. If the person consents, wonderful!

If she hedges, you may add that you are interested in finding out how she is doing, and that you don't intend to stay long. If she consents, great!

If the answer is still negative, don't be too quick to back down. Remain friendly, and say something appropriate, such as: "We used to run into one another now and then. I'd like to visit for a few moments to see how you are doing."

If she still declines, you may have to accept that verdict gracefully. Express a good wish. However, don't consider that the end. One early evening, stop by the person's house unannounced, and say, "Hi, I would just like to say in person that I care about you." She may be taken aback a bit, and you may sense an awkward moment of silence. But remember that the kingdom of heaven has often come in moments of such silences. Chances are that they will respond with grudging appreciation and may even invite you in. Remember, don't stay long; this is just a "say hello" call.

With a vision for this ministry, the facts in hand, and an initial contact behind you, you're ready to make a get-acquainted visit. We'll talk more about this visit and follow-up visits in sections five and six.

Points to Ponder

- When you became an officebearer were you aware of the facts about membership loss in your church? What surprised you?
- Has your council caught the vision for this ministry? What role can you play?
- How have your responsibilities toward the members under your care affected your personal devotions? How are you growing in love toward the members in your district? Do they sense this growth in you?

Section Five

The Get-Acquainted Visit: Building Bridges

Alone or As a Team?

Should you make the get-acquainted visit alone or as a team of two? Both have advantages. Two know more than one and can support each other, but going alone may be less threatening to the person receiving visitors. One-on-one interaction is more conducive to building a trusting relationship. It's easier to guide the conversation in a chosen direction without wondering what a teammate will say. In general, the pastoral calls I've made alone have been more effective.

With that advice, let's visit with a single gentleman whom we'll call Andy. No one's seen Andy around your church for half a year, probably longer. Your initial phone contact has been mildly successful. Andy agreed to have you stop by. The moment of that first visit has now come. You make your way to his house, say a little prayer, and ring the doorbell. Andy opens the door and ushers you into the living room. The get-acquainted visit has begun. How do you proceed?

A Visit with Andy

Remind yourself to relax. Your goal for this visit is simple; it's to become acquainted with Andy, not much more than to say "hello" in person.

Observe the setting in which you find yourself with Andy. Make some appreciative comments about Andy's house, his nice garden, and so on. Inquire about Andy's health or about his family. Inquire discreetly about his background, perhaps even his likes and dislikes. You may also ask about his work, particular gifts and ideals, possibly plans for the future. If Andy shares some problems with you, show due interest but let him tell his story. Take note of Andy's body language. Does he seem tense? Or is he warming up to you a bit? Try to say something that will put him at ease.

Andy will probably not broach the topic of church attendance. Neither should you. Remind yourself that you came to become better acquainted. You are interested in how he is doing. You will communicate with Andy on his terms. Only then will you begin to build the trusting relationship needed to minister to Andy on an ongoing basis.

SMALL TALK?

You may be tempted to begin your visit with some harmless small talk just to "break the ice." Think twice. Disadvantages far outweigh advantages. Once sidetracked by small talk, you face the awkward task of pulling the discussion back to the purpose of your visit. A better way of breaking the ice is to inquire sincerely and thoughtfully about the well-being of your host. The information gathered will help you greatly in your mission.

Be an attentive listener. Tune in to Andy. Make mental notes of some things that seem important to him. When there is a short lull in the discussion, and if you think Andy has already shared several matters with you, announce that you must leave. Thank Andy warmly for his hospitality. Ask if there is anything that you can do for him. Shake his hand, express good wishes, and ask if you may stop by again in the near future.

Assessing the Visit

Think back on the visit. How did you do? Chances are you did better than you perceive. Andy will very likely find himself appreciating your visit. Often people who have become estranged from the church don't have many friends. You've shown an interest in him, something Andy may not have experienced for some time.

Thank the Lord for this opportunity, and pray that this initial get-acquainted visit may lead to something bigger. Next, write down the significant points of the visit:

- What were the main things Andy told you?
- Did any concerns surface that seemed important to Andy's well-being?
- Is he perhaps worried about anything?
- Did he boast about anything?
- How do you think Andy feels about you?

It's important to make a tentative determination about the reason Andy left your church. Read section three (pp. 31-35) once more. Did Andy leave for internal reasons? External reasons? Interpersonal reasons? Institutional reasons? Your subsequent visits will be affected by this initial judgment.

Finally, try to evaluate your own emotional response to the visit. If you were at all a bit afraid or nervous, don't let that bother you. Visits are not always easy. Did you find some anger in your heart? Put it in the hands of the Lord. Are you pessimistic about Andy's spiritual future? Remind yourself of the power of the Holy Spirit, to whom you owe your own salvation and who can create life out of dry bones (Ezek.37:7-8).

Other Scenarios

Andy's response as described above is the best of several possible scenarios. Andy might have responded more negatively. He might not have said much at all. You still need not regret that you used this low-key approach. You have preserved your own dignity, and you probably left Andy in a better frame of mind. At your next visit, that may become evident.

It is also possible that Andy told you in no uncertain terms that he considered himself no longer a member of the church and that you need not visit him again. Even in such a situation, suggest to Andy that you would like to come back to arrange the formal conclusion of his membership. Always be on the lookout for arranging one more visit. Who knows? It may just lead to further explorations and still one more visit. And who knows how the Spirit will use your patient perseverance? Those who were once with the church become an urgent evangelism prospect.

Running into Anger

Among the disaffected members, some will be angry at the church or some members of the church. They may voice that anger to you in no uncertain terms, even at this initial short visit. How can you best deal with it?

Remember that in many cases, the people you visit have not had an opportunity to express their anger in a protected setting. Bottled anger can be potent. Since you represent the church, it may seem to be directed at you personally. In spite of that,

Your purpose in this first visit should be bridge building. Those of us who are goal conscious find that difficult. We prefer the direct approach: "Why don't you come to church anymore?" Such an approach is usually premature and will rarely be fruitful if a trusting relationship is absent.

In small churches or small communities where people know each other well, this circumspect approach may seem unnatural. The one visited will not be in doubt about the purpose of your visit. In such situations, it is better to bring up the matter of church membership and Christian commitment during the first visit. Even then, it's still important to inquire about the host's well-being and to show due sensitivity to possible problems, burdens, or pain.

- Do not defend yourself or the church.
- Do not argue.
- Give a person ample opportunity to explain his or her anger.
- Ask questions for clarification.

You may show your empathy for the pain such persons usually have. But express neither agreement nor disagreement with them. Guide the ongoing conversation toward a better and clearer understanding of their grievances. (See also section nine where conflict is considered in more detail.)

Finally, remember that the presence of anger has a positive side. It may well be an indication that such members still care about God and his church, even though they are now stuck at the far end of a detour. Stick to your strategy; let them tell their story and try to win their confidence. You are their friend, not their adversary. You are a bridge builder. Try to look at situations through the lenses of your hosts. Try to arrange the next visit. Most changes of mind and heart take place in between visits.

Keep It Short!

A get-acquainted visit should be kept under half an hour. Remind yourself again that the initial visit has a limited purpose. Your ministry to this party will come in stages, a bit at a time. It is the long maturing process that leads to healing. The Lord himself will determine when fruits are to be harvested.

Points to Ponder

- Think back to your very first get-acquainted visit. Did the visit go better than you expected? Worse than expected? Why?
- As you've made more get-acquainted visits, have you grown in self-confidence? What factors have contributed to this? What tips would you give to someone new at this?
- Have some visits left you with regrets? Or wishing you had said more, but didn't because of fear of rejection? Or wishing you hadn't said something?
- Have you received the brunt of anger in any of your visits? How did you feel? What did you say or do?
- Did you find it hard to keep visits within reasonable time limits? What are some of the reasons visits become too lengthy? What effect does this have on building a trusting relationship?

Section Six

The Follow-Up Visit: More Than Process

Ongoing Ministry

Suppose you have completed two get-acquainted visits with a person on your list and you are reasonably sure that a trusting relationship is forming. How will you proceed?

You must now plan the follow-up visit. In this visit, you will zero in on the person's relationship with God and seek to minister to his or her spiritual needs. Many of the principles and practices will hold true for most visits—though it must be said that no two visits are alike. They are mostly full of surprises.

Let's make such a visit together. But first a word about the approach we will use.

Our Approach

Kenneth Haugk of Stephen Ministries advises that in ministry to those he calls "inactive members," the visits should be *process* oriented, not *goal* oriented. Haugk, in his book *Seventeen Keys to Effective Ministry to Inactive Members,* defines these members as those "who have chosen not to participate in worship life, financial support, and the program activities of the congregation."

Process-oriented ministry emphasizes listening and waiting patiently in an honest attempt to enter sympathetically into the inactive members' minds and situations. These visitors identify with their subjects and accompany them for a while on their journey. Success is not their immediate aim, although it may be an end result.

In goal-oriented ministry, visitors tend to come with an agenda. They want to solve a problem or rectify a situation. The visitors will use rational arguments in order to change the inactive members' minds. They will argue for a certain course of action or change of behavior. And they hope for success from their own point of view.

During the 1990s, and perhaps before that, the process approach was widely favored, possibly to a fault. It fit the mold of those who sought to avoid normalized counseling. And, indeed, for our follow-up visit, it is wise to use the process approach for relationship building.

But those who visit on behalf of Christ's church go beyond the process approach. They must speak the mind of Christ, who not only lovingly understood people's plights and the kingdom's slow growth, but also told sinners to sin no more and to do the will of the Father (Luke 8:1-15; 13:18-20; 15:11-32; 24:13-35; John 4:5-26; 8:1-11).

So in dealing with disaffected church members, show forbearance and patience as Christ was forbearing and compassionate. Let them tell their own stories. And at the same time, remember that Christ was honest and direct. To the woman whom the Pharisees brought to him to see whether he was soft on sin, Jesus said, ". . . neither do I condemn you. . . . Go now and leave your life of sin" (John 8:11). Jesus said, "Blessed are the merciful" (Matt. 5:7), but he also said that he had to come to call "sinners to repentance" (Luke 5:32).

A THREE-STAGE VISIT

In order to build relationships and reach out in Christ's name, you will find it helpful to arrange your visits around three stages:

- Stage One: Invite your party to talk about himself or herself. Focus on the person's well-being and life situations, events, experiences, and other details.
- Stage Two: Inquire how the realities of life have affected the person's emotions. For example, you might ask, "How did you feel when . . . ?"
- Stage Three: Bring God into the picture gently. For example, you might ask, "Could you pray about your situation?" or "Did you sense that someone was praying for you?"

Your ongoing concern in all three stages should be to build a relationship. Enter into the situations of those you visit, listen to their stories, and work at understanding their perspectives. Keep the discussion on track, and avoid any kind of unrelated small talk such as sports, politics, road repair, and so on. And remember to keep your visits reasonably short. (About one hour is best for these visits.)

In successive visits, move through these three stages again, allowing the third stage to become more prominent in your discussion. As you develop a spirit of trust, this will become easier to do.

ONE DOESN'T ALWAYS FIT ALL

Life is seldom so neat and predictable that it readily submits to our preconceived designs. It may well be that before you can implement the three-stage process as described here, your host refers to the purpose of your visit. "So much for process," you say to yourself.

But to come to a visit without some concept of how to construe your mission is far less desirable. Even if you find that the process doesn't seem to fit a particular situation, you will likely experience that even the most unpredictable visit will offer opportunities to ask about your host's well-being, feelings, and relationship with God.

A Visit with Hannah

Hannah went through a divorce some years ago and since then has not attended church very often. You've made a couple of brief visits to become acquainted with her. It is clear to you from those visits that her life is not easy. She has traveled through deep valleys. She has many problems, and you wish you could help her find solutions. You also wish that you could bring her back to the Lord.

Even though you sense that Hannah is open to a follow-up visit, you are even more aware of your own limitations. But you've scheduled a visit—it's time to go. Let's see how the three-stage approach can work for you.

STAGE ONE

It's important that you focus on strengthening the bridge of confidence. Hannah probably has few listeners in her life, so she doesn't mind telling you about her experiences. She will probably defend herself a bit. Don't interrupt her except to ask for clarification if you need it. As you listen and focus on her, affirm her as a person. She finds in you a fellow traveler, if only for a short distance. Don't allow yourself to judge her (Matt. 7:1-4; Rom. 2:1-4). She has likely already judged herself and received the same from others. As you piece the bits of information together, you begin to see her story unfold, privileged to catch a glimpse of a modest human drama.

STAGE TWO

You must determine at what point Hannah has completed her story. Now you try to communicate with her on a bit deeper level. You might say,

"That must have been a very painful time for you." Or ask, "How did you feel when you sensed rejection from people at church? Have you been able to sleep or keep up at work?" You have now invited Hannah to open up her heart a bit and to give you her subjective responses. You can follow up by asking, "How did you cope?" or "Have you been able to talk with a friend about this?" Listen carefully to what she says. Be patient. This is precious time. As emotions enter in, tears may begin to flow; they help greatly in the communication process.

STAGE THREE

Now you can bring God into the picture—but not abruptly. You might ask if Hannah was able to pray in the situation she's shared. Perhaps she will share that she was unable to pray. Without implying that she should have prayed, encourage her to see that God is a very present help in trouble. God wants us to come to him with all our cares.

You have now helped Hannah to connect her plight with her spiritual condition. She may gradually come to see that her own responses to her trials and perceived injustices are part of the burdens she carries. Without accusing or rebuking Hannah you have led her to see that she needs to take some responsibility for her situation. Only the patient kind of caring penetrates defensiveness.

You must remind yourself that a visit such as this can probably do no more than help Hannah (and you) take a small step forward on the road to spiritual health. Always avoid trying to accomplish too much in one visit. More will happen once you leave. Hannah will think about what you said, and what she said, and how she felt as you visited. Hopefully this visit is one of several to follow; your ministry to Hannah is still in its beginning stage. So it's better to conclude the visit gracefully and to suggest that, perhaps, Hannah would agree for you to come back soon. Use your judgment if the moment seems right to make an appointment right then. Otherwise wait a week or so, give her a phone call, ask how she is doing. Then suggest setting a time for another visit.

Finally, keep in mind that much of the pastoral work done with those at odds with the church tends to seek correction, improvement, change, and repentance. Although it's unavoidable, this more goal-oriented ministry can leave a negative feeling with those you visit. Each visit will assume a more positive flavor if you weave in some "appreciative inquiry." Ask about a person's gifts, ideals, skills, hopes, plans, and goals. You may then encourage a person to develop and pursue those with good hope. You may also find that these discussions will cement your relationship with the one you seek to help.

Assessing the Visit

However your visit may turn out, write down the details as soon as you come home.

- What, if anything, stood out?
- How would you assess Hannah's mood?
- Thinking back about the four reasons why people leave the church (see section three), which one would fit Hannah best?
- Is there anything you can already do for her?
- What suggestions would be helpful for a future visit?

Pray for Hannah regularly. Ask the Lord to bless the visit. In a few days, send Hannah a note of appreciation and your assurances of prayer.

Schedule successive visits fairly close together, probably no more than one or two weeks apart. The more time elapses between visits the less effective your ministry will be. In between visits, review your notes, pray for the person daily, and ask for wisdom.

Other Scenarios

Admitedly, we've described the visit with Hannah as a "better case" scenario. It is very possible that Hannah would not be nearly as willing to visit with you and that she would be less forthcoming in sharing her story with you. Alas, "worse case" scenarios do occur frequently in this broken world. Every visit begins where you find a person. Take heart in the knowledge that your gracious listening (process) approach with Hannah will probably leave her in a better frame of mind. She may just feel some admiration for the church because you sought her out and were ready to listen without correcting or condemning her.

Although it's probably unlikely, should Hannah inform you on the spot that she wishes to resign her church membership, suggest that she think it over. Indicate that you would like to come back and discuss the details with her. When working with disaffected members, remember that the more brief visits you can slip in, the better!

Points to Ponder

- Reflect on *process-oriented* ministry and *goal-oriented* ministry. Do you favor this distinction? How might the follow-up visit with Hannah have gone if it had been more goal oriented? What would happen if subsequent visits only followed process orientation?
- In what other areas of your life might this distinction between process and goals be helpful? How could you use both the process-oriented approach and the goal-oriented approach with your teenage children? At work? In council meetings?
- In a visit resembling the one described in this section, did you feel sympathy for the member? How did you deal with disagreeable elements in the discussion?
- Have you ever tried to arrange a visit and it was refused? How did you feel? What might you have done differently?

Section Seven
Visiting Those Who Leave for Internal Reasons

Who Are They?

Who are the members who leave their churches for internal reasons? They are those who have not come to faith in Christ. Doubt has eroded their conviction that God exists, or that God can be known, or that God needs to be served. They have heard the Master's call but have not surrendered to him. They don't feel the need for the Savior who gave his life for sinners. If they do struggle with guilt, they don't take it to Christ.

Some of these people may become angry opponents of the gospel, but it is more likely that they quietly go their own way and gradually distance themselves from the church. They may give themselves to an overt sinful life (Jude 4; Rom. 1:21), but more often they are virtuous people who simply don't believe (Luke 18:18-25; Acts 17:19-23).

A Visit with Kay

The person whom you are about to visit is Kay Young. You have visited her briefly twice before. Kay's parents are longtime members of your church, and they are concerned about her spiritual well-being. Kay left town several years ago for college and graduate school. A year or two ago, she returned to her hometown to teach at the local community college. She attended church a few times with her parents, but you have not seen her in church for more than a year. Kay has agreed to visit with you, though probably somewhat reluctantly, and you meet in a restaurant at the edge of town. You'll apply the three-stage technique again.

STAGE ONE

You ask Kay if she is pressed for time, and she assures you that she has two hours before her next class. You remind yourself that the success of this visit does not lie in the cleverness of your reasoning; in fact, you realize that Kay is probably smarter than you are. But you also realize that with all her gifts, Kay is a human being dependent on God—who may have great things in mind for her.

Kay soon realizes that you are an interested listener, and she finds herself telling you about her work. She appears to enjoy teaching, although she notes that the world of learning has plenty of problems. You will probably enjoy this visit. Kay is a nice person with a fascinating life. You ask her about the problems to which she alluded, and she shares some details with you. You commend her gifts and achievements. You ask about her ideals and goals.

STAGE TWO

Next, you intentionally zero in on some deeper concerns that you feel sure are also part of Kay's life. You can get at issues such as happiness, fulfillment, and personal ideals in different ways. For example, you may say that you have heard that students struggle with issues that go beyond learning; they're fearful and searching for meaning and purpose in life. You might ask Kay if such issues have been part of her contacts with students. Does Kay address such issues in her classes? Kay may be a bit on her guard now, uncertain about what you are aiming for; but don't back off too easily. Note carefully what she says. She must now speak a bit more from her heart. You may proceed by asking if she herself has struggled with such issues.

It is hard to predict what direction the discussion will take. Try to keep on course. Don't feel hesitant or wonder whether the topic is proper. Kay is a strong woman; she is fully able to give an account of her convictions. Her response will help you ease into stage three of your visit.

STAGE THREE

You may ask Kay whether it would not seem reasonable that God is part of these human predicaments. Kay may venture some answers. Note them carefully. And then take the next important step, a step you must not avoid. Ask if it would seem reasonable that Kay, as a person and as an academician, would recognize such a God in her life. Discussions are always unpredictable, but you will likely engage Kay in a discussion about God—perhaps whether God exists, whether God can be known, whether

God is involved in the world, whether God has opened a way of reconciliation in Christ, and whether God invites us to be his followers. Remind yourself not to argue; you ask, suggest, and, most of all, listen.

The discussion may take an unexpected turn. Kay may turn the table on you. She may say that if God is Creator and Provider, how can he permit such terrible suffering in the world? Why doesn't God come to the rescue of abused children or protect the defenseless?

> Among the people who have left the church for internal reasons will be several who have given the Christian faith considerable thought. They may well be good readers. Your church should have books on hand that may help them in coming to a better understanding of salvation. (See titles by C. S. Lewis, Philip Yancey, and Lewis Smedes listed in the Bibliography.)

A number of things cross your mind. You don't have all the answers. If it weren't for God's grace, you would think much the same way Kay does. And you have plenty of moments in your life that you have your own doubts. This may well be the opportunity to express your humble testimony that you have experienced doubt, guilt, forgiveness, and a relationship with Christ. This relationship is precious to you, though you admit that it not always equally strong. Peter reminds us to give an account of the hope that is in us (1 Pet. 3:15); Paul did it in grand style before the governors Festus and Agrippa (Acts 26:24-26).

If time permits, you may round out the discussion by pointing out that trying to explain life without God also produces problems. How can reality be explained without a wise Creator? What is the source of goodness and beauty, if not God? Why do our hearts cry out for good relationships and acceptance? Why do we feel the need to resolve guilt? How is it that throughout history human minds have been occupied with the divine? Ultimately, what is the meaning of life without knowing God? A universe without God is a scary place.

All the while, you carefully avoid sounding strident and argumentative. You are not out to win an argument. As you and Kay express opposing points of view, *do not see Kay herself as your opponent.* Let your deep spiritual concern for Kay be your restraint. Let it be evident that you listen to Kay with interest. You can learn from her. You are privileged to have this fascinating visit. Thank Kay for her willingness to give you so much of her time. Wish her well in her personal and professional life. Suggest that you would like to visit with her again.

Assessing the Visit

Once at home, write down pertinent points of the discussion. Thank God for the visit. Ask the Spirit to give the increase. Search your heart for weaknesses in your approach, and ask the Lord to provide wisdom.

Send Kay a note of appreciation. If Kay is inclined to talk more with you, schedule the next visit within a couple of weeks. You will find that there is still much to talk about. Follow the three stages; discuss her well-being, her inner response to life's realities and struggles, and whether she is still thinking about God. The outcome is in the hands of God. You are only the instrument. Do not worry about "success."

Other Scenarios

It is also possible that Kay would not be very willing to visit with you. Kay may well have made up her mind about the faith of her youth and have no wish to pursue your mission much further. Still, if you could somehow get her to consent to your coming once more, use the opportunity gladly.

You don't know what the Lord has in store for Kay. But if she will not agree to visit, propose that you will still stop by for a moment and arrange with her how her membership in the church can best be terminated. The advantages of such an arrangement will be yet another visit and a member that is released with care and dignity. God may someday use the memory of your compassion to stir her faith once more.

When visiting people who have left for internal reasons, you will have moments that you feel depleted and overwhelmed. Your task is indeed a daunting one. Do not hesitate to use other resources in your Christian community. In Kay's case, ask her if she would like to visit with your pastor. You may also suggest that she join a seeker's group or other small groups composed of thoughtful Christians. Or perhaps you know of another member who has had experiences similar to Kay's who would invite her to attend church and discuss the sermon and worship with her afterward.

Points to Ponder

- Have you known people like Kay? How did you feel about visiting with them about spiritual matters? If not, how might you rewrite the scenario described to fit your comfort zone?
- Have you had doubts about your own faith? How did you deal with them?
- How would you respond to a son or daughter who told you one day that he or she didn't believe in God? If you have experienced this or know others who have, what is the best approach to take?
- What is the difference between discussing the faith and arguing about it?

Section Eight

Visiting Those Who Leave for External Reasons

Who Are They?

Those who leave the church for external reasons find their delight in areas of life disconnected with Christian living. They may cement friendships with people who have no interest in Christianity. Or they devote so much of their time and resources to personal entertainment that church life is gradually crowded out. The Bible calls it "worldliness" (John 17:25; Rom. 12:2). When this becomes a way of life, such members will probably stop attending church altogether.

As a district elder, your list may contain one or more names of people who "love the present world" (2 Tim. 4:10). Ministering to them is not easy. The gospel tells us that their worldly pursuits are like thorns that choke out the seed of the Word (Mark 4:19; Luke 8:14).

A Visit with Bob and Beth Park

The young couple you must visit are Bob and Beth Park. Although they are members of your church, they have not attended for almost a year. You've paid them two brief get-acquainted visits and sense that they were not eager for you to come. You feel that their absence from church is connected with their lifestyle. Bob and Beth travel a lot and go boating on Sundays. With some anxiety, you prepare for a follow-up three-stage visit.

STAGE ONE

You begin the visit with the tried and true, inquiring about their well-being. You ask about their work, their families, and so on. When Bob and Beth wander off, try to keep them on track. And keep in mind that the clock is ticking.

STAGE TWO
Soon you dig a little deeper. You ask

- Have the good things of life created peace in their hearts?
- Have they become thankful people?
- Have they become better people?

Bob and Beth hedge in their answers. Keep in mind that people in this category don't readily deal with issues of the heart. They deal with life in practical, concrete terms. That's why it may be best to proceed to the third stage rather soon.

STAGE THREE
Make a reference to the Lord. Have Bob and Beth been able to share their good times with the Lord? When problems arose, did they take their burdens to him? Do not rebuke them for their negligence; rather, assure them that we can be patient when things go against us, and thankful when things go well. We can trust our faithful God and Father.

It's also possible that Bob and Beth may in passing refer to some fortunate things. Dwell on them a bit. Ask some follow-up questions. What are their fears? What are their plans for the future?

Be slow to remind the Parks that returning to church would be a good thing for them. When you sense that you have covered as much ground as is helpful in one visit, express your appreciation for their hospitality. Suggest that you would like to make an appointment soon for another visit.

Assessing the Visit

Review the visit and make a record of what transpired. Reflect on the things Bob and Beth talked about. Pray for yourself and for the Parks. Assess your feelings. Were you impatient with this couple? Did you misspeak yourself? Don't fret about these weaknesses. Make some notes of pertinent points and highlights in the conversation. As always, schedule visits fairly close together.

Remind yourself that the real change of heart for Bob and Beth must come from the Holy Spirit. They will reflect on what you discussed, the questions you asked, and what they heard from each other's mouths. They have probably not discussed their drifting away from God much. That kind of reflection during the subsequent days does far more than your urging them to return to church. Their eventual return to your church will only be a reflection of their becoming living members of the Body of Christ. At this point, rebuking them for their lifestyle is not helpful. Keep your eye on the goal: the Parks must reconsider their relationship with God.

Other Scenarios

Suppose that the Parks are more positive and cooperative in this visit. Suppose that they express some regret or admit wrong. You may then assure them of God's forgiveness. And you may broach the matter of church membership and the need to worship with God's people. If they are very positive, you may suggest the next Sunday morning. You may even offer to accompany them. But don't insist. Be on the lookout, and should you spot them in the church foyer, welcome them, introduce them to others, take them to the coffee fellowship after the service.

Further follow-up visits will still be essential. In due time, you may invite the Parks to share in some church activities. Perhaps you can think of other members who might invite the Parks to come to church with them, stay for a meal, or accompany them to a suitable group activity. God has wonderful blessings in store for his servants. But remember, God sticks to his own timetable. Good things most often come slowly.

On the other hand, it is also possible that Bob and Beth would have been far less accommodating. Already a little ways into the visit, you realize that their hearts are not with the Lord and his people anymore. You realize soon that your options are more limited. Again, you focus on the Parks' well-being. You show interest in their lives. You show your concern for them as people and listen carefully to what they tell you. You follow up on what they say.

Then you ask how their life experiences have affected them. Do they feel happy, sad, afraid, angry? Bob and Beth will have to account somewhat for their feelings and reveal some of their personal needs. They may squirm a bit, trying to evade your questions, changing the subject. But continue the theme. Were they able to talk together about their feelings?

When responses remain sparse, the time is ready for you to give your own modest testimony. Avoid telling stories or incidents about yourself, but share that in similar situations you found strength in the Lord and comfort in prayer. You need not do much more than that unless unexpected opportunities arise. In a situation such as this, do not broach the subject of church attendance. What matters is that you've left a simple message that Bob and Beth must find their way back to God.

Points to Ponder

Have two elders role-play follow-up visits with Max and Rose:

- Max, a single young man in your elder's district, is a member of the local police force. You've missed him in church. After several phone calls, you have an appointment to visit him. On this first visit, Max tells you that his demanding duty roster makes it hard for him to attend church. As you refer to his faith and commitment to the Lord, Max admits that church means little to him and that the few Sundays he is off duty are better spent in rest and relaxation. What will you plan to say at a follow-up visit?
- Rose is a nurse in a local hospital. She seems to have given up church attendance. On your first visit, Rose tells you that budget cuts have reduced the nursing staff and that she works long shifts. She admits that she's bone tired when she comes home. She also adds that she grew up in a very strict family and that she and her sibling were forced to go to church twice each Sunday and attend every possible church activity. Rose tells you that church life has become a burden to her. What will you plan to say at a follow-up visit?

Section Nine

Visiting Those Who Leave for Institutional Reasons

Who Are They?

Members who leave for institutional reasons have problems with the ministry program of the church. Or perhaps they resent certain elements of the Sunday services. If they join another church, the leadership of your church should make an effort to talk with them—conduct a sort of "exit interview." Perhaps your church can learn from them and make corrections. When such members fail to join another church and discontinue attending altogether, the church must reach out to them with ongoing pastoral care.

A Visit with Phil and Mary Baker

Phil and Mary Baker have not been in church for three months. Their adult children grew up in your church, and although their membership has been low-key over the years, they were considered loyal members. You are their district elder.

You recall the details of the get-acquainted call you made earlier. Since you considered the Bakers to be empty nesters you had dropped by unexpectedly one early evening, and they had invited you in. That visit was a bit uncomfortable, but at least you were able to assure them of your goodwill, and they seemed to appreciate your interest in them. Somewhat abruptly, Phil had mentioned that they had not attended church for some time. When you inquired about the reason, Phil was evasive, mentioning only that the services just hadn't done much for them and that they were working on some issues. You offered to return soon to discuss their concerns and they agreed, though somewhat reluctantly.

You used the intervening time to consult the notes you made of the get-acquainted visit. You also phoned the previous district elder, who told you that the Bakers are very private people. On one occasion, they had been critical of the church. With these facts in hand, you're ready to try the three-stage technique in a follow-up visit.

STAGE ONE

Begin this follow-up visit with a few words of appreciation for the Bakers' hospitality. Avoid small talk, and break the ice by focusing on them. Inquire about their health, children, jobs, and so on. Note whether they repeat details of the previous visit. If so, their comments may indicate a worry, fear, or disappointment. Pursue it a bit to determine what issues Phil referred to in your first visit. When what they say makes sense, nod your understanding; or, if appropriate, express your sympathy. When you cannot fully understand, ask for clarification.

STAGE TWO

You may ease into stage two by asking the Bakers if they have been able to discuss any of this as a couple. Did they agree in their assessment of things? This is an important part of the visit. Follow through on how the issues they've shared have affected them.

STAGE THREE

Move cautiously into stage three. Have Phil and Mary been able to pray about these issues? You may find that the Bakers are hesitant about expressing their emotions. You cannot change that. They may feel that you are pressuring them a bit. Don't let that bother you. These are the kinds of moments that open the way to a substantive discussion. And all of this is a good way to set the stage for broaching the subject of their relationship to the church.

Be on the lookout for several possibilities. Are they displeased with only a segment of church life? From your point of view, is their problem something that can be remedied? Is what they object to of an organizational nature? Or the ministry practice? Or the worship services? The sermons? The teachings of the church? Have they suffered personal disappointments? Allow the Bakers to explain themselves in detail so that you get a clear picture of their difficulties with the church. Try to determine whether they harbor anger or resentment.

At this stage, listen. Ask follow-up questions for clarification and for showing your own interest. Don't argue. Do not become impatient. If their observations are obviously incorrect, you may venture a corrective clarification, but be modest. The Bakers have probably given the whole matter more thought and observation than you have. At any rate, avoid argumentation.

You have some choices at this juncture. You may discuss the objections the Bakers have against the church, perhaps inviting them to explain themselves some more. You may inquire whether the Bakers themselves have some proposals the church may consider. You may also propose that you may try to remedy the problems they have pointed out. But be careful that you don't load too much into this visit. In a visit such as this, you cannot do much more than listen carefully to what the Bakers have to say and give them the assurance that you will look into it. You may also ask their permission to discuss their concerns with the elders.

Assessing the Visit

As you reflect back on the visit, you wonder whether the Bakers' criticism has validity. You are a loyal member of the church, and you may find it hard to appreciate their criticism. But churches are not perfect.

Set steps in motion to investigate the perceived imperfections. Perhaps you and your fellow elders are able to address some of the Bakers' concerns. You can then discuss this with the Bakers at your next visit. If what they object to are matters of style or taste, you may wish that they could be changed for their sake, but style and taste are elusive. Changes may not satisfy the Bakers; they still may insist on leaving the church.

Other Scenarios

It is also possible that already at this visit Phil and Mary inform you that they have made up their minds about leaving the church. They find their problems with the church just too formidable, and they have no hope that solutions can be found. In such a case, try to schedule another visit. Explain that church membership is of great importance, and resignation should not be made lightly. If they consent, you will have another opportunity to explore a better solution with the Bakers.

If the Bakers are adamant and announce that they want to leave your church, suggest that you would like to visit once more to arrange formal resignation. It is important that the Bakers' leaving be done amicably. More importantly, this will enable you to make sure that Phil and Mary will join another Christian church. Remember that members who become disenchanted with the church may visit here and there, but often end up attending nowhere. Your ministry to the Bakers is to make sure that they find a home in another church.

Points to Ponder

- In response to a report of a visit such as the one to Phil and Mary, some elders show little sympathy for members who are critical of the church program. Others support their desire for a viable program. What arguments could you think of in support of either?
- Elder Myers has a hard time with the changes that were made in the church's ministry program. One day he decides to visit Elder Cooper, who favored the changes. Role-play the discussion between the two leaders.
- What will it take to convince the Bakers to join another church? If you were welcomed for a "resignation" visit, how might you facilitate this new membership?

Section Ten
Visiting Those Who Leave for Interpersonal Reasons

Who Are They?

Those who leave for interpersonal reasons leave because they are at odds with other members of the congregation. Conflict can be between individuals (member and leadership, member and member, and so on) or between segments in a congregation. Both types of situations cause grief, bad feelings, and pain. Both require careful pastoral care.

A Visit with Del and Deb Green

Let's consider the hypothetical case of Del and Deb Green, who have had a falling-out with Shane and Sarah Hoff. The Greens feel offended by what the Hoffs are reputed to have said about them. The relationship between the two couples has now become strained. The Greens feel more deeply about this unfortunate development than do the Hoffs. The strained relationship has puzzled the Hoffs; they find the incident unfortunate, but they are prepared to leave it behind them. The Greens feel hurt, and it bothers them that the Hoffs seem to be casual about it. The Greens have confided in other people, and the conflict is now in the open.

The Greens decided to stop attending church and other activities. You found out later that they withheld their financial contributions too. These developments were brought to the attention of the pastor, who asked you, their district elder, to visit the Greens. Your schedule was full, and so it was not until a few weeks later that you phoned them to make an appointment. Since you have known the Greens fairly well, and since some weeks elapsed before you made the appointment, you decide to dispense with the get-acquainted call. You'll follow the three stages for your visit.

STAGE ONE

You begin your visit by inquiring about the Greens' well-being. Since their well-being is closely tied to the conflict with the Hoffs, they soon refer to it. And they add the comment that it sure took the church a long time to note their absence. Be careful not to defend yourself or the church. Aggrieved people experience perceived lack of concern as another painful offense. And often in a case like Del and Deb's, husband and wife enforce each other's feelings of indignation. Allow them to add details as they see fit; be prepared for many. People in painful conflicts often replay the details over and over in their minds.

UNDERSTANDING AND ASSURANCE

Disagreement and conflict among church members bring deep pain to the participants. Only they themselves can truly understand. The visitor will be confronted with the details of the conflict, probably even sooner than described in the visit with the Greens. The irony is that the visitor's sympathetic understanding—without expressing agreement—must be a prominent ingredient of the visit. These members must be assured that, no matter how complex and unfortunate the situation, they belong to the family of believers.

The Greens now proceed to build their case. Continue to listen attentively. It will occur to you over and over that the Greens see the situation totally from their point of view, that they are not very charitable, and that they judge the motives of their perceived antagonists frequently. They appear not to take responsibility for anything they've said or done. But remind yourself that all this is typical of people who have been caught up in conflict and bear the pain of it. Do not try to correct them. You must hear the whole story the way the Greens need to tell you.

STAGE TWO

At some point you will recognize that the Greens have more or less finished their account. You must make some comments. Thank them for feeling free to trust you with these details. Tell them also that you realize that they have had a difficult time. Be careful not to express agreement. If you do, you will be quoted later with some exaggeration. And do not express disagreement. If you do, you will lose their trust, and further ministry will be hampered. Since visits of this type tend to focus on the negative, listen for something commendable, and perhaps comment on it.

STAGE THREE

In a visit of this type, you may find it wiser not to switch to stage three. Most likely, the Greens simply need to be heard this time around; they (and you) are probably not ready to try to figure out where God fits into all of this. Instead, suggest that you would like to reflect on what the Greens have told you and come back for another visit. By now you will likely have spent an hour, if not longer, with the Greens, and you're sensing that wisdom is in short supply. Leaving at this point will likely have a positive effect. The Greens may begin to see the conflict in a different light. They may not realize it, but something has happened to them by telling the details. They will think about what they've said. They may well be a little less convinced of their case. They may feel a bit embarrassed, having expressed themselves so adamantly. At any rate, they will likely be somewhat more open to your subsequent input than if you had stayed and pursued it for hours into the night.

Assessing the Visit

As with the other visits we've considered, write down details of your visit. Note especially what seemed inconsistent to you in the Greens' report. And during subsequent days, do some research about this conflict. As you think about the Greens' story, do you begin to see some avenues or alleyways that could lead to a resolution? Continue in prayer for the Greens and for God's blessings on your work. In the meantime, don't wait too long to make an appointment with the Greens for the next visit.

The Follow-Up Visit

Prepare yourself carefully for the follow-up visit. Begin the visit with good hope. Conflicts can be solved, though not always. It is also good to remember that the conflict is not your fault. Do not assume responsibility for the conflict itself. If the Greens address you with some vehemence, let it slide off. Even in the presence of the Greens' anger, remain your gracious self in Christ.

How to proceed at this second visit depends a bit on how you find Del and Deb. Are they more relaxed than last time? Chances are that they are. They have told you their story at some length, and they may wonder how you feel about them and what you will do. You may begin by expressing your appreciation for the previous visit. You may observe that you have thought and prayed about what they told you and that you understand that these are difficult times for them.

From here, proceed cautiously. If you think that the Greens may be receptive to it, you may request their permission to visit with the Hoffs to explore how they feel and whether they are prepared to visit with the Greens. Keep in mind that this would be quite a step for Del and Deb, but also for Shane and Sarah Hoff. Explain to them the advantages you see. Try to remove their fear. You may also explain that a meeting of parties at odds is in keeping with the Lord's will as laid down in Matthew 18.

Caution the Greens that they must not come to such a visit to score a victory but to seek mutual reconciliation. Tell them frankly that conflicts always have many sides to them. The Hoffs have their points of view too. They must be given an opportunity to give their clarifications, something the Greens may find helpful.

"SUCCESSFUL"?

When members leave the church because of interpersonal conflict, elders will be inclined to focus on reconciliation. That would solve the problem, and you as an elder would be "successful." The course of action for the follow-up visit as described above fits this pattern. But we must remember that our primary focus should always be the spiritual well-being of the parishioners. Don't hesitate to point out that only in the center of God's grace can those in conflict come to terms with their anger.

If the Greens accept that suggestion, you can offer to arrange a meeting with them, yourself, and the Hoffs. Interpersonal conflicts are generally best resolved with a mediator.

If the conflict is not resolved, the Greens may decide to leave the church. Keep an eye on them. It is very important that they leave in as good a spirit as possible. Continue to drop by for short visits. Urge them to join another Christian church. In this vulnerable time the Greens are in danger of becoming disconnected from the body of Christ altogether. But with your help they just may join another church. At one of your subsequent visits you may propose that they find it in their hearts to forgive the Hoffs.

Congregational Conflicts

In the case of a broader congregational conflict, the battle casualties can be many. In this situation, you will work in tandem with your fellow elders and pastor(s). Focus on the spiritual well-being of the members who are drawn into the conflict. Some of your members will experience real despair and grief. Anger will surface. Minister to them in and with the love of Christ. Plead with them to be patient. You may point to the apostle Paul, who was patient with the churches where several parties were at each other's throats (1 Cor. 10:1 -17).

Generally churches with conflicts wait too long before inviting outside conflict specialists to assist them in finding reconciliation. Less than half the churches struggling with broad conflicts actually engage the services of professional mediators. The irony is that the leaders themselves often form the barrier; they are afraid that the mediators will not see things their way.

Some churches will try to ignore the conflict or smooth it over without addressing the underlying issues. Then those who need personal pastoral care will not get it, tensions remain, and the exodus of members is inevitable. Those who leave are often so disillusioned that they do not join another church. The church from which they have come will not do much follow-up care because the elders are too tired and discouraged. The classes of such churches should not hesitate to step in and make resources available to reach out pastorally to those lonely members.

Members of churches that have moved through conflict should be visited over and over, especially those who were drawn into the proceedings. Popular wisdom tells us to move on and forget what lies behind. Spiritual compassion tells us otherwise. Go and see the troubled members; ask them how they are dealing with their pain and whether they can lay it in God's hands. And keep praying!

Points to Ponder

- How would you handle the following conflict? (In your meeting, role-play the scene with two elders playing the farmers and another serving as the mediator.)

  Nick Mulder decided the time had come to take life a bit easier. So he asked Case Nobel, a fellow church member and farmer living nearby, if he wanted to rent the "eighty," a nice plot of land suitable for growing soybeans. Case felt the price was a bit steep, but indicated that he was interested and would like to think it over. A month later, Nick's nephew offered to pay a half year's cash rent on the spot. Nick accepted the check that sealed the deal. When Case heard about it, he was very upset. "You promised me the land," he said. "No, you promised to let me know, but you didn't," Nick replied. As the conflict intensified, Nick's and Case's district elders succeeded in getting them to meet with a mediator.

- An elder, somewhat impatiently, contends that the current conflicts in the congregation are symptomatic of a spiritual malaise. He urges the pastor to address this problem more forcefully from the pulpit and call the congregation to repentance. What elements, both pro and con, might be part of the council's subsequent discussion?
- What support services are available to your congregation should conflict between segments of the congregation mushroom into unresolved conflict? What denominational resources are already in place for you to access?

Part Three

Preventing Members from Leaving Their Churches

In this section, we will explore some steps a church can take to prevent members from leaving. We will see that a church can do a lot to keep members from heading for the "back door." But we will also see that the church cannot—nor indeed should it—bar the door shut. The health of a church has many aspects. That's why a church has several ministries, each ministry contributing toward a church's well-being. When members are nurtured and challenged, they tend to remain loyal to their church. However, a church cannot always meet the needs of all its members. Some will indeed flourish better elsewhere. And some will not respond positively to the gospel. No matter how painful, the church must let them go, not from the heart but from the membership rolls.

Section Eleven
Church in a Big World

Church and Society

Society is the scene of a complex interaction of forces and ideas. Life is uncertain for the strongest of us. Bread earners know the fear of unemployment. Business people know that insolvency can steal upon them unawares. Corporate greed has squandered fortunes and ravaged the pension funds of aging workers. The evening news focuses on destruction and violence. National economies are uncertain. Relationships between countries are volatile. The world seemingly can't get much worse, but yet it steadily does. And so people weave cocoons around their fragile existence.

Maintaining our families and our selves—building our cocoons—demands all our energy and resourcefulness. Families are busy. Parents work to buttress their economic base. Common meals happen less frequently. Peer pressure forces children to place more demands on parents. Believers often lack time for personal devotions. Family devotions have become less common. Family time is squeezed out. Being nominated for a church office becomes problematic. Many are too tired to attend worship each week. Life's incessant demands cause chronic fatigue.

This trend may be intensified by the philosophy of individualism that has pervaded society. The counseling industry, though concerned about constructive relationships, focuses on the well-being of the individual. Many psychologists resent the churches' communal value system. Self-actualization and the "be all you can be" philosophy have contributed toward a pleasure-seeking life style. Freedom without norms is in.

These societal values and mentalities have made their inroads into the church. Cultural realities affect all of us as members. Day in, day out, the church is exposed to society's values, ideals, temptations, and cultural patterns and trends. In their hearts, believers would like to experience their church as an island of safety and goodness surrounded by the wilderness of society. But that is not always a reality. As human institutions, churches have their shortcomings. They cannot be all things to all people. Inevitably some members are disappointed in their churches. Many of the empty places in our pews were once occupied by people whose needs and pain were not recognized by fellow church members.

Consumerism

In the late 1960s and early '70s, a new generation came on the scene. The "Baby Boomers," born between 1946 and 1955, brought the age of consumerism. They also left the churches en masse. Churches and their leaders responded by redoubling their efforts to win new members for the faith.

To their credit, churches developed a plethora of imaginative methods of evangelism to aid in this process. As with all new methods, not all were Spirit inspired. The consumerism that drove the Boomers out of the churches crept into the churches. Churches learned how to meet a great variety of needs in order to make bigger gains in membership influx. New members did join in large numbers. Thank God! But it is also true that many "converts" made a rather quick exit. They became "reverts." The "back door" designation was born.

What can churches do to remedy this sad course of events? Solutions are not easy to come by. Churches must increasingly become attractive communities of grace. They must also increasingly become prophetic communities, proclaiming the gospel of repentance that is not always popular. Through the grace of Christ and the power of the Holy Spirit, members must be equipped to serve each other and to enfold newcomers. Churches must become communities of love.

The Church as a Community of Love

Among all the human communities in society, the church occupies a most remarkable place. The church is more truly *community* than all the others. Selfless love binds members together, making them an organism. Believers are members of the Body of Christ. Thus they have a connection like no other. Restored to God, they live as covenant partners with him. This love of Christ enables believers to live a peculiarly balanced life. As if stabilized by two poles, they

- seek to receive but also to give.
- need to be nurtured but also to be challenged.
- cherish closeness but also personal space.
- bring correction but also know when to stand back.
- make honest inquiry but also know when to listen.
- stand up for the truth but also know when to be tolerant.
- defend their God-given rights but also recognize when to be the least.
- reach out to help but also to be helped.
- confront when necessary but don't withhold forgiveness and acceptance.
- sometimes criticize but don't hold grudges.
- practice transparent openness but always respect privacy.
- grieve but are not given to anxiety.
- belong but also maintain their individuality.
- trust their neighbors but with a touch of sobriety.
- avoid dependency but consciously seek inter-dependence as responsive members of a loving community.
- praise God for creating the day for work and the night for sleep.

Church communities grow in maturity as individual members become adept at living this love-balanced life. Relationships are dignified and gracious because the members respect and honor each other's individuality but will also contribute to the community's common good. No matter how strained and confused relationships may sometimes become in a community, such believers will continue to accept responsibility for each other, all the while respecting each other's individuality. (For more insights on these thoughts, see Peter L. Steinke's books listed in the Bibliography, p. 109.)

The apostle Paul spoke eloquently of that unity in these words:

> The body is a unit, though it is made up of many parts; and though all its parts are many, they form one body. So it is with Christ. For we were all baptized by one Spirit into one body. . . . If the foot should say, "Because I am not the hand, I do not belong to the body," it would not for that reason cease to be part of the body. And if the ear should say, "Because I am not an eye, I do not belong to the body," it would not for that reason cease to be part of the body. . . . The eye cannot say to the hand, "I don't need you!" And the head cannot say to the feet, "I don't need you!" . . . Now you are the body of Christ, and each of you is part of it.
>
> —1 Corinthians 12:12-31

The transformation of churches to such communities of love comes through the preaching of the Word with fervent prayers for the Spirit's blessings. But good leadership can enhance the process immensely, for two reasons:

- first, because leaders can model this love-balance in their personal conduct and in their leadership styles.
- second, because leaders can clarify this underlying love pattern.

Church leaders can explain to the membership how underlying relational patterns function. They can show the members in what ways their backgrounds are helpful to them and what ways detrimental. In the presence of widespread anxiety, they can demonstrate the security that believers may claim in Christ. Leaders can deal with opposition in honesty, not afraid of confrontation, but always in the peace that the presence of Christ unfailingly affords them.

Understanding this vision of the church as a community of love is very important in ministry to those who are becoming estranged from the church. On the one hand, some may experience the closeness of believers as oppressive. Leaving the church feels like relief to them. On the other hand, there are some who feel isolated in the church. They feel distant from other members, unworthy of a respected place. They think they don't count. They don't feel valued. For opposite reasons both these groups feel isolated. Neither experiences love and fellowship.

That's why, in ministering to a person who is disconnected from your church, careful observation is so important. Caregivers can only hope to be a blessing by first getting to know the person they care for. Try to understand the reasons for the disaffection. Make several visits. Without a relationship built on trust, you will not be able to understand the person's needs and the way he or she related to fellow members.

The more a congregation resembles Paul's picture of the church as the body of Christ, the more the atmosphere becomes inviting to lonely members. They will experience concern and acceptance without feeling corrected and rebuked. They will feel closeness without being pressured. Expressions of love and concern will not be suffocating.

In Romans 12:13 Paul writes, "Contribute to the needs of the saints, extend hospitality to strangers." One missionary whom I interviewed told me, "We try daily to love people into the kingdom." Such ministry must be intentional. With careful thought and prayer, churches can become winsome, attractive, thoughtful, friendly, and concerned communities. In such communities, lonely members will find growing companionship. Young families with problems will find solace and help. Children and young people will find a meaningful place and know themselves challenged. The elderly will be appreciated and valued. In such loving communities, the members are aware of each other's needs, and all help all.

At the same time, such communities of love and concern are not perfect. The irony is that churches, eager to attract new members, have a tendency to portray (advertise?) themselves as communities of perfection and excellence. But most often people are looking for a church that has a hospital-like quality: a group of fallen, struggling people who can sympathize with others who have been wounded by a harsh society (Matt. 9:12; Luke 5:31). Yes, churches *are* mosaics, beautiful only because broken pieces are fit together into a design of grace (Eph. 3:13-16).

The Church as Redeemed People

Amid all the aspects of busy church life that demand our attention, it is important to keep in mind what the church really is. The church is a community of people loved by God and loving God. They are God's redeemed. Together and individually they relate directly to God in Christ Jesus. That relationship is strengthened by three main things:

- ministry of the Word.
- the practice of godliness.
- Christian fellowship.

These three are not ends in themselves; rather, they point believers to God.

But what has happened all through history is that the focus has shifted from God

- to the teaching and preaching about God.
- to the service of God.
- to the loyalty of the community of God.

Faith has become grounded not so much in God himself as in teaching, service, and togetherness. The result has been a spirituality that has lost some of its focus.

In church communities where living in God's company is the going concern, members will be blessed. Surrounded by a harsh society they, with fellow members, will find solace before the face of their God. There they will find encouragement and meaning in a secularized world. There they will find renewal and assurance to remain faithful to God during the week ahead. There, hope is deepened to continue in loyalty to God. Such churches afford their members a lifeline to new spiritual vigor. Where this is not so, members will stay for other motives: social advantages, community approval, friendships, or agreement with doctrinal views they find reassuring. But these other motivations are not unchanging; "certainties" of that sort have a way of evaporating. And then members have no solid reasons to maintain their memberships.

In the next few chapters we must explore these implications a bit more. What can the church do to help members live in God's company?

Points to Ponder

- In a get-together of some leaders of your church, ask them to describe in a few sentences their relationship to the membership of the church. How have these relationships been shaped by family backgrounds?
- What evidence of "chronic fatigue" (see p. 75) do you see in your church membership? Think especially of its effect on recruitment of volunteers, Sunday attendance, participation in midweek programs, and so on.
- What are some things that could be done to deepen the spiritual life of the members? What can be done to strengthen relationships, prayer life, the ministry of mercy, worship services, Bible study, evangelism, fellowship, hospitality, and so on?
- What evidence can you give that your membership understands the needs of the neighborhood around your church? What steps could your church family take to get to know the neighborhood and for the neighborhood to get to know you? Is this a prominent concern of your deacons?
- What can the council do to promote and strengthen a sense of community in your church? (See list on p. 77.) How will members and those you hope to bring in recognize this in you? How will you identify those who aren't experiencing community?

Section Twelve
The Ministry of the Word

Much has been written about preaching. We'll focus here on some aspects of Word ministry that appear to have an impact on keeping members with the church.

Bring Christ

Pastors must remind themselves of the reality that some people in the pews have no relationship with the Lord. Some experience a clouded relationship with the Lord. Some are burdened with doubt or troubled by broken relationships. All need the gospel; all need to be encouraged and challenged. As pastors prepare their sermons, they do well to picture these people in their minds. Will each one meet Christ through the message?

Make It Relevant

The message should be relevant. It must address members who face the relentless demands and stubborn problems of today's society. The stress of society is not foreign to pastors, and members must sense that their pastors have walked a similar road during the week. Sermons must reflect some of today's events and realities; they must not sound as though they could have been preached decades ago.

Be Engaging

Sermons will be engaging and winsome if pastors address their congregation as if they were seated across from them at the kitchen table. One pastor whom I interviewed said, "As I write my sermon, I ask how my message would strike my daughter who has left the faith." Another said, "I look over my congregation of people from all walks of life and I ask if my sermon will specifically touch their hearts and be meaningful in their daily lives as parents and children, teachers, painters, doctors, and so on."

The more a sermon focuses on the covenant, the more engaging it will be. Covenant is togetherness: God, brothers and sisters, and their pastors. In the Spirit of Christ, pastors will feel secure enough not to scold their congregation from the pulpit, not to feel afraid of power brokers, and not to be angry at perceived detractors. Richard Baxter, the great Puritan preacher of Kidderminster Parish of Worcestershire, Massachusetts, once said that people are saved and sanctified by a pastor's demeanor more than by the sermons. Congregations tend to emulate the personalities of their pastors.

PARTNERS
Time spent by pastors visiting parishioners is time well spent. Pastors are shepherds who lead and feed. They are also partners with their parishioners.

Explain The Lord's Supper

The Lord's Supper does two things for believers. The sacrament

- *portrays* salvation so that it becomes more meaningful to them.
- *seals* salvation so that it becomes more certain to them.

The Lord's Supper is Christ's special provision for the New Testament church to strengthen its members in their journey. The Lord's Supper does not add anything to the salvation believers have in Christ; it adds to the *certainty* with which they experience that salvation. Partaking of bread and wine assures believers that it is so!

Followers of Christ must not doubt that they are forgiven and that they belong to Christ whom they confess as Savior. Believers meet their Christ at the communion table. The liturgist must remind the partakers that they are the guests of Christ the host. The holy supper is a meal. Believers feed on Christ's grace. As bread and wine strengthen and quicken the body, so the believers' faith is nourished.

Note also that believers attend the supper together. It is a fellowship meal. They eat of the one bread and drink of the one wine. They experience unity and togetherness. Pastors would do well to explain this to the congregation. Elders should now and then encourage their pastors to prepare holy communion in such a way that the congregation has a clear understanding of what happens and what their partaking means to them (Rom. 14:1; 1 Cor. 1:9).

Points to Ponder

COME

Doubt and loneliness are two factors that often play a role in members' leaving the church. The Lord's Supper addresses both.

- Pastor Jim asked the elders and deacons to meet once a month to discuss his sermons and the way they are preached. What are some of the benefits? What might be some pitfalls?
- When have you last encouraged your pastor? Who pastors your pastor?
- When did you last express some sustained interest in the life and activities of a member of your district? How can this help to foster a sense of walking the faith journey together?
- Do you think communion should be served more often or less often in your church? Why? What can be done to make the sacrament more meaningful?

Section Thirteen

The Church's Pastoral Care Program

The Core of Pastoral Care Ministry

The strength of a church's pastoral care program lies in an elusive but pivotal goal—creating an atmosphere of spiritual growth. Church services, budgets, classes, sermons, liturgies, events, lectures, discussion groups, education programs, youth ministries—and the list goes on—must bring people to Christ, deepen their relationship with Christ, and increase their knowledge of his Word.

The temptation for church leadership is to tend the church's organizational aspect at the expense of spiritual pursuit. Churches indeed deserve to be well administrated and to have well-appointed programs. But those should always be means to an end. When the focus shifts from spiritual essence to organizational flair, the church can become an obstacle to the coming of the kingdom in the hearts and lives of the people. I once heard a preacher say, "When successful programs and events receive admiration and commendation beyond the borders of the local church, chances are that they may assume an idolatrous place in the hearts of church leaders."

The church leadership must ask if programmatic diligence is given more weight than the quest for godliness. In true spirituality lie the bonds that bind believers together in Christ. The unity of a congregation is not so much grounded in friendships, common ethics, and common interests as it is in its closeness to Christ.

Perhaps we may turn that around. When that unity loses its spiritual core and when members then become disappointed with the program and the community, they may well leave and see if other settings afford them the same friendships, recognition, and interesting activities. Or they may join another church that has more appealing programs. And this may trigger a trickling away process.

The people of Israel followed that pattern centuries ago. The prophet Hosea proposed: "'Let us acknowledge the Lord; let us press on to acknowledge him'" (Hos. 6:3). But the people's hearts were not with the Lord. Speaking though Hosea, the Lord asked, "'What can I do with you, Ephraim? What can I do with you, Judah?'" (v. 4). The outcome was predictable: "'Ephraim is like a dove, easily deceived and senseless—now calling to Egypt, now turning to Assyria'" (7:11).

COMPASSION

Jesus told the parable of the lost son:

When he [the son] came to his senses, he said, ". . . I will set out and go back to my father and say to him: 'Father, I have sinned against heaven and against you. . . .'" But while he was still a long way off, his father saw him and was filled with compassion for him; he ran to his son, threw his arms around him and kissed him.

—Luke 15:17-20

Spiritual Leaders

Throughout its history, the Christian Reformed Church has emphasized that a primary responsibility of the church's leadership is providing pastoral care for the membership. Article 12 of the *Church Order* states: "[The pastor], with the elders, shall exercise pastoral care over the congregation." Article 65 adds further details:

> The officebearers of the church shall extend pastoral care to all members of the congregation and to others whenever possible by calling and encouraging them to live by faith, conducting annual home visitation, seeking to restore those who err in doctrine or life, and comforting and giving assistance in adversity.

The form for "Ordination/Installation of Ministers of the Word" says:

> The minister of the Word is called, together with the elders, to shepherd the people of God in the Christian life, guiding and counseling. . . . They are pastors, appointed to shepherd the church of Christ which he purchased with his own blood, in keeping with the Lord's command: "Feed my sheep!"

—*Psalter Hymnal,* 1987, p. 996.

The form for "Ordination of Elders and Deacons" (*Psalter Hymnal,* p. 1004) makes similar provisions for elders: "Elders are thus responsible for the spiritual well-being of God's people. . . . And they must promote fellowship and hospitality among believers. . . ." They are charged to "bear up God's people in their pain and weakness, and celebrate their joys with them."

The apostle Paul told the Ephesian elders to "keep watch over yourselves and all the flock of which the Holy Spirit has made you overseers. Be shepherds of the church of God which he bought with his own blood" (Acts 20:28). Paul told Timothy to "set an example for the believers in speech, in life, in love, in faith and in purity" (1 Tim. 4:12). Elders are challenged to be "shepherds of God's flock that is under your care, serving as overseers . . . being examples to the flock" (1 Pet. 5:2-3).

When the officebearers maintain imaginative contact with the members assigned to them, they will pick up the first signals of a spirit of malaise among them. They can then approach such members with their best ministry efforts. Elders and deacons, with the pastor, can survey the congregation at worship and take note of those who are not present there. One elder whom I interviewed told me that he carries with him a list of names of the members of his district at all times. When he misses some of his members in the services, he sends them a copy of the bulletin with his best wishes.

The spiritual leaders of the church have a beautiful but also a difficult task in their churches. Their own godliness and dedication to their task will add so much to the quality of their ministry. Billy Graham and his associates published the well-known *Modesto Manifesto* in l948. "Leaders," it said, "must be known for their honesty, integrity, purity, and humility."

Diaconal Ministries

Next to the ministers and elders, the deacons can also minister to those who struggle with their church membership. Their mandate is very diversified.

A well-functioning diaconate will enrich and sweeten church life. It will provide an element of trust and acceptance that marginal members need to experience in order to be drawn closer to the center. The "Form for the Ordination of Elders and Deacons" (*Psalter Hymnal,* p. 1004) challenges deacons to

- relieve victims of injustice . . . desiring to give life the shape of things to come.
- assess needs.

- promote stewardship and hospitality.
- collect and disburse resources for benevolence.
- develop programs of assistance.
- speak words of Christian encouragement.
- demonstrate the care of the Lord himself.
- exercise their office with prayer, patience, and humility.
- teach [the congregation] to be merciful.
- prompt [members] to seize new opportunities to worship God with offerings of wealth, time, and ability.
- realize that benevolence is a quality of our life in Christ.
- minister to rich and poor alike.
- be compassionate to the needy.
- encourage [the needy] with words that create hope . . . and with deeds that bring joy.
- be prophetic critics of the waste, injustice, and selfishness in society.

Diaconal work, when imaginatively conducted, will add to the church's ministry activities. These ministries may have a special appeal to members who have concluded that the church makes little difference in the world. When such members can be recruited for some of these activities, they could well be energized and motivated to practice what the church preaches. In his book on the work of deacons, Jay Van Groningen (see Bibliography, p. 109) makes helpful suggestions as to how

- Christian ministry can be effectively balanced, focusing on people both inside and outside the church.
- gifts, talents, skills, and resources of church members can be employed to bring meaning and well-being to the people in the neighborhoods around the church.
- the root causes of needs can be discovered.
- local churches can bless wider neighborhoods.
- churches can partner with other institutions for the common good.
- needy people can be restored to dignity in Christ and find a respectful place in the Christian church.

For additional direction regarding diaconal ministry, see Article 25, Article 76b, and Article 77b of the Christian Reformed *Church Order* and *Acts of Synod 1987,* pages 618-619. Read Paul's reference to deacons in Philipians1:1 and Acts 6:1-7.

Ministry to Loved Ones Around the Empty Pew

Parents and other close relatives of those who left are probably grieving, mostly in silence. As a caregiver, seek them out and sit down with them for a quiet talk. They will share some details with you. Your role is to listen without giving advice. Loved ones of those who left struggle with a painful reality surrounded by a profound mystery. They will appreciate your praying with them. Ask the Lord to bring the wandering back to faith and for the Lord to comfort the loved ones.

The loved ones may ask you whether they must continue to witness to their wayward child or sibling. That is a difficult matter. The following scenario may be of some help.

REACHING OUT TO TRICIA

Suppose Tricia, a single twenty-year-old, attends church less and less. One day she announces to her parents, Rod and Marge, that she doesn't want to be a member of the church any longer.

Her parents engage her in a conversation. They avoid anger, argumentation, accusation, wailing, panic, and preaching. They ask Tricia to tell how she came to this decision. They may ask whether something they did or didn't do contributed to her leaving. It is important that this conversation not end in blaming and distress. Rod and Marge listen patiently and assure Tricia of their love and prayers. Perhaps older siblings will be part of this conversation; they give the same assurance.

Rod and Marge and other members of the family continue to talk about their faith, church matters, and kingdom activities, much as before. The tone and tenor of family life remain the same—they are church people. Tricia will probably not mind. She is used to it anyway and will probably feel relieved that family life is not conducted under the pall of sadness and avoidance.

WHERE CHRISTIANS MUST BE

I simply argue that the cross of Christ must be raised in the marketplace. I am recovering the claim that Jesus Christ was not crucified on an alter between two candles, but on a cross between two thieves; on the top of a garbage heap; at a place so cosmopolitan that they had to write his name in Hebrew, Latin, and Greek; at a place where cynics talked smut, thieves cursed, and soldiers gambled.

That is where he died, and that is what he died about, and that is where Christians must be.

—G. McLeod

Rod and Marge will wonder if they should continue to "witness" and confront Tricia. Sometimes an opportunity may present itself. They will then avail themselves of that. But generally they will remember that their primary relationship to their daughter is that of parent and child. They will concentrate on being the best parents they can be. They will be careful to keep the lines of communication wide open. They want to create an atmosphere that is inviting to Tricia. She will want to come home because she feels at home. If Tricia begins to feel threatened, she will avoid coming home.

Tricia's parents have two things going for them. They have given their daughter a Christian upbringing. They need not add much to that anymore. And they know the power of prayer. The rest is up to God's sovereign love.

As their spiritual counselors, you may help parents in similar situations to adopt a strategy such as this. Assure them that God's Word will accompany their children wherever they go. Parents must also realize that the spiritual wanderings of wayward children are likely to create some guilt in their hearts. Anxious admonitions addressed at their children may well be the result. Encourage them to place that guilt into the Lord's hand and to be assured that God's grace will prevail.

A MOTHER'S ACCOUNT

My daughter Julie and I have always been close. She was never close to her father. As a teenager, Julie grew away from the church. That really upset her father. He would often tell her to mend her ways. She gradually avoided him. In her late teens, Julie left home and stopped going to church.

Whenever she came home, my husband always drilled Julie about her church life. It created a lot of tension. I once told my husband not to bring up the church issue every time, but my husband said that it was his duty as a parent to warn her.

Every time Julie came home, I felt caught in between. Now Julie doesn't come home much anymore. Her father rarely mentions her name. Julie and I keep in touch mostly by phone. I cry a lot.

Timely Ministry

One of the dismaying things about losing members is that their exit is often discovered too late. The memberships of larger churches are often scattered over wide areas. From the moment that worshipers drive away from their churches, they will not see most of their fellow members again till the following Sunday.

Church leaders have to find imaginative ways of keeping members in contact with each other through the week. Only then will the quiet slipping away of members be lessened. Researchers found that the reason most often given by young families for leaving their churches is that they had problems and no one took note. The sooner the officebearers observe that some members are no longer attending the church services, the sooner they can contact them.

But I hasten to add: members too must also minister to each other. Article 79 of the *Church Order* states that "members of the church are accountable to one another . . . and have the responsibility to encourage and admonish one another in love." Officebearers must "instruct and remind the members of the church of their responsibility and foster a spirit of love and openness within the fellowship. . . ." I can't think of a more perfect formula for preventing lonely members from falling through the cracks.

Small Groups

The harmonious unity of the community of believers has often been enhanced by the formation of small groups. Though small group ministry is a modern phenomenon, John Wesley (1703-1791) pleaded for small group formations. He called such groups *societies*; they were further divided into *classes* composed of as few as four believers. He urged participants to "watch over each other in love." Today we call it *mutual accountability.* Paul himself profited from sharing his needs with believers (Phil. 4:10-15), and he frequently pointed out how much Christians need each other (Rom. 12:3-8; 1Cor. 12:12-30).

Small groups assume various forms and function in different ways. In small groups, newcomers find listening ears and accepting hearts. In small groups, seekers find a sense of belonging; they find the soul of the congregation. Real ministry takes place. Those with needs are connected with resources. Fears, doubts, misgivings, and pain are addressed. It is often in small group settings that those without hope, ready to drop away from the church, are given the embrace that keeps them within the fold.

The Stress of Change

Officebearers must also be aware that progress cannot be made without change. But change is often upsetting to some members. Change comes with risks. Officebearers themselves may oppose change because they know that some vocal members feel uncomfortable with it. But when change is necessary to meet new needs and challenges, the church leadership must not hesitate to see it through at the risk of criticism and opposition. In the absence of progress and change, stagnation will set in and enterprising members will leave.

That holds also for the worship services. Gospel preaching must remain the core of the services, but the response of the members in prayer, praise, testimony, and song must also be a meaningful part of church services.

When members leave at a steady rate, churches must take a good look at the quality of their overall ministry programs. Perhaps we can learn from other evangelical churches that are growing right along.

THANKS!
Communication is more than information dissemination. It is also the sympathetic expression of appreciation to all who toil in the church's program.

Communication

This book is not about communication, but we must emphasize that communication plays a significant role in congregational health and well-being. Faulty communication invariably leads to misunderstanding and confusion. Strained, even broken relationships will result. They, in turn, play a large role in members leaving churches. Communication needs to be handled with intent, forethought, grace, accuracy, and timeliness. Announcements and information regarding events, programs, and policies usually bear repetition. The old adage "What can go wrong will go wrong" is more often true about communication than anything else in the life of the church.

Church leaders can facilitate the communication process by

- informing each other of activities they have observed or of which they have been part.
- discreetly sharing the needs and problems of members who may benefit from the help and prayers of fellow members in their district.
- sharing details of the overall ministry program. Events need to be announced clearly and later on be reported to the membership.
- informing members about decisions and proposals that the leadership makes.

Points to Ponder

- How can your council members be good stewards of your church's organizational life and still remain deeply aware that the essence of church life is a personal love relationship with God?
- What can you do personally as a spiritual caregiver to humbly portray that your love for God and God's people is primary?
- Do you agree that there is no growth without change, but change comes at the price of discomfort and stress? What evidence of this have you seen in your church?
- What are some practices you could adopt to maintain good contact with the members of your district? How can you encourage them?
- How can you prepare to visit families in which a member no longer attends church?
- In your meeting, one council member states that since most of his district members now meet in a small group that he attends, calling on members at their homes is no longer necessary. Others disagree. What do you think?

Section Fourteen

The Role of Youth Ministries

Strategic Importance

Churches concerned about the membership drain will devote much care to their children and young people. When younger members leave they most often leave quietly. They will not readily make their wishes known to the leadership. Those who leave without joining another church will probably become the parents of families without church connections.

Some of the children of the Baby Boomers are coming back to church. The type of ministry that appeals to them is similar to what appeals to youth already in the church. Imaginative youth ministry takes motivation, skills, and resources. Give youth work a prominent place in your ministry program and the budget. Promote it from the pulpit.

Most churches have youth elders or specially trained youth ministers. And the commendable work of GEMS, the Calvinist Cadet Corps, and Youth Unlimited are well known within the Christian Reformed Church. District elders and church school teachers should always keep close contact with the youth elders and youth pastors regarding the well-being of the church's youth. Here too teamwork is of the essence.

A Sense of Belonging

Acceptance by peers is of crucial importance to youth. Young people have a sense of and need for belonging that differs from older members. One youth leader whom I interviewed told me that young people's experience of belonging is akin to tribalism. The Boy Scout movement actually uses such terms as *pack* and *group*. Youth seem to relate to these terms.

Another youth leader whom I interviewed adds an interesting observation. She found that the majority of young people who participated in the church's music program stayed with the church. Involving youth in the church's ministry activities will indeed contribute toward their feeling of belonging and thus their loyalty to the congregation.

A SACRED CHARGE
"Be a friend and Christ-like example to children. Give clear and cheerful guidance to young people."

—"Ordination of Elders and Deacons," *Psalter Hymnal*, 1987, p. 1005

Personal relationships are affirmed in the way of such little things as leaders knowing the names of individual children and young people. Being informed about their well-being and details about their lives will mean a lot. One young person told me: "We have a man in our church who knows the names of all of us kids. I guess he memorized them all." The more personal attention young people receive (in a quiet, low-key manner), the more likely they will stay with the church.

Young Adult Ministries

Our young people in higher-learning institutions face an uphill spiritual battle. Christianity has lost its standing in secular universities. The person and teachings of Christ are relegated to the realm of the mythical. "Christian ethics," I heard a university pastor say, "are readily associated with intolerance and hypocrisy." Local church leaders must go out of their way to keep in touch with their members studying in distant places. Campus ministry begins in the local church.

The CRC Campus Ministry has greatly contributed toward maintaining a Christian presence at secular campuses. CRC churches are now bringing a form of ministry to some forty campuses across Canada and the United States (twenty-four of those are supported by CRC Home Missions). The Campus Ministry office has drafted several helpful documents and position papers that students can use with profit. Information and ministry helps may be requested from the Campus Ministry director (U.S.: CRC Home Missions, 2850 Kalamazoo Ave. SE, Grand Rapids, MI 49560; 800-266-2175; Canada: Box 5070 STNLCD, Burlington, ON L7R 3Y8; 800-730-3490).

While some young adults may be reached by campus ministries, others, especially those who choose employment over college, may not be reached at all. A retired minister made an observation worth noting. He pointed out that the one segment of youth ministry that receives little attention in most churches is the post-high-school group composed of those who have graduated from high school but have not yet married. This pastor said, "The churches just don't invest much in the formation and training of that group. In my experience, it is from this group that we lose many." Church leaders take note!

OUR CHILDREN—
THE FUTURE IS HERE!

The Commisson on Children at Risk presents a challenge to families and churches. Their research shows that

> The weakening of authoritative communities is a principle reason . . . why large and growing numbers of children are failing to flourish. . . . Strengthening these communities is likely to be our best strategy for improving the lives of our children, including those most at risk.
>
> Essentially, science is increasingly demonstrating that the human person is hardwired for close attachment to other people, beginning with father and mother and extended family and then moving out to the broader community. . . . We are hardwired to connect to other people and to moral and spiritual meaning, the transcendent. . . .

—"Hardwired to Connect: The New Scientific Case for Authoritative Communities," *A Report to the Nation*, Institute for American Values, New York, NY, 2003

Points to Ponder

- What percentage of your total church budget is earmarked for youth work? Should it be higher? Lower?
- In what ways is your congregation regularly informed about details of the program?
- Does your council have a system in place that provides for regular briefings with youth leaders and teachers? If not, what system can be implemented?
- Do council members know which of your young people live in distant places as students, soldiers, professionals, and so on? What provisions have you made to enhance contacts between them and the congregation?

Section Fifteen
A Final Question

We conclude with this final question:

Can the back door exodus be slowed down?

From one point of view, yes, the trickling away of members can be halted. From another point of view, no, it cannot always be prevented.

Yes

The foregoing pages have been written in good confidence that churches can do a lot to keep members from leaving.

Is your church willing to have a close look at its ministry programs and ask if they are effective and useful? Is Christ central in your ministry program?

Ministry programs need to be assessed constantly. They need to be pruned and augmented. The challenge toward renewal is never finished. Sometimes influential members obstruct efforts toward wholesome change. Sometimes church leaders become shortsighted, set in their ways, impatient with those who suggest new initiatives. When churches develop blind spots toward better and timely ministries, good members will leave. Corrections take effort. Where your church seeks to serve the Lord faithfully, members will not leave easily.

The answer to the problem of members leaving their churches lies, in many cases, in upgrading ministries without moving an inch from their scriptural foundation. Sometimes upgrading means no more than that the spirit in which ministries are done is being ennobled. Ministers and elders should take an interest in the work of the many volunteers, encourage them, and express their appreciation in tangible ways.

No

But resignations are not always preventable. Today, perhaps more than before, we see a great deal of variety in believers' faith experience. Differences are numerous. Good members join another Christian church because they honestly feel they can worship and serve there better. Every time this happens, a church must evaluate the reasons and see whether it can make improvements and corrections or take new initiatives.

But the church will also realize that there are limitations to such efforts. Churches must acknowledge that they cannot be all things to all people. We believe in the universal Christian church. We thank God for other Christian congregations that provide ministry for which they are better equipped than we are.

As we've noted, it is far more painful when members leave their church because in their hearts they have left the Savior of the church. Some of those may be in disagreement with the core teachings of the church. The church tries hard to bring them to repentance, but when it is to no avail, they have in the end no choice but to acquiesce in their resignations or to terminate memberships.

Rely on the Spirit

As churches seek to minister to their members, they find themselves deeply dependent on the Holy Spirit. The Spirit lays out the spiritual journey for each of Christ's followers. Some of the greatest saints of the Lord have come to their spiritual destiny via painful detours, some of which are beyond their understanding. Christian caregivers, together with Christian parents, hope for a journey that leads straight to commitment to Christ and joyful service. And that is the church's ministry's aim! But sometimes it happens that the Lord leads along a different road. Blessed are those church leaders who labor in deep trust that this will come to pass in the Spirit's time and in the Spirit's way.

Points to Ponder

- Someone in your council meeting says, "No matter how hard I work, no matter what new methods I use, ministering to God's wandering sheep is hard work. Sometimes I feel I just cannot go on." What can you do to encourage this coworker?
- In what instances have you found the advice in this book helpful? What were some instances for which this booklet failed to prepare you? What might have helped in these situations?

TELL US!

We'd like to hear how this book helped you in your ministry. And we'd like to know in what ways it didn't prepare you for the tough task of caring for those who leave. Please contact us at

Faith Alive Christian Resources
2850 Kalamazoo Ave. SE
Grand Rapids, MI 49560
Phone: 800-333-8300
Fax: 616-224-0834
E-mail:
editors@faithaliveresources.org

Appendix

On Church Discipline

Most Christians value their church membership. They treasure it as a privilege. Members of Christian Reformed churches are no different. When they joined their church through a ceremony known as *public profession of faith,* they affirmed that they

- believe in Christ as Savior.
- hold the Bible to be the true Word of God.
- accept the promises of redemption as expressed in their baptism as infants.

And they responded to a fourth question: "Do you promise to submit to the government of the church and also, if you should become delinquent either in doctrine or in life, to submit to its admonition and discipline?" ("Public Profession of Faith," *Psalter Hymnal,* 1987, p. 963). The form for "Baptism of Adults" has a similar question (p. 968).

The form makes it clear that membership implies a serious obligation. When members are no longer willing to assume responsibility for their membership, the church will surround them with ministry aimed at helping them overcome the obstacles to a fruitful, viable membership. The Christian Reformed Church made this a central concern in its *Church Order.* Article 65 mandates that the officebearers bring pastoral care to the members, *"seeking to restore those who err in doctrine or life."*

But the *Church Order* did more. Article 79 expands that ministry significantly. It states that members are *accountable to each other and that they owe each other ministry.* They must "encourage and admonish one another in love." The same article then adds that the officebearers "shall instruct and remind the members of their responsibility."

It is only when this ministry from members to members does not produce results that the elders of the church assume a more prominent role in the process of restoration. They will make a set of visits pleading with erring members to return to the Lord. They will do this with great patience, realizing that life is complex and that error is often intertwined with other complications in those members' lives.

ARTICLE 79

"The consistory shall instruct and remind the members of the church of their responsibility and foster a spirit of love and openness within the fellowship so that erring members may be led to repentance and reconciliation."

—*Church Order of the Christian Reformed Church*

Article 78 of the *Church Order* spells out the purpose of this ministry. It is not punitive but, rather, its purpose is "to restore those who err to faithful obedience to God and full fellowship with the congregation." The Christian Reformed synod of 1991 (see *Acts of Synod 1991*, pp. 265-67; 720-23) affirmed this noble goal of members ministering to members and the restorative role of the elders when such ministry is not successful.

Jesus referred to a situation that is obliquely related to the above. He said: "If your brother sins against you, go and show him his fault between the two of you. If he listens to you, you have won your brother over. But if he will not listen, take one or two others along. . . . If he refuses to listen to them, tell it to the church . . ." (Matt. 18:15-17; see also *Church Order* Articles 80-81).

Synod emphasized that such ministry processes be conducted with patience, fairness, and magnanimity. It also spelled out a set of guidelines so that predictability, uniformity, and truthfulness are guaranteed. Investigations must be thorough and impartial, and those involved should be given every opportunity to state, explain, and defend their case. Where this does not lead to repentance and faithful church membership, the elders will have no choice but to continue this process of church discipline. At a certain point, the elders will advise such a member not to partake of the Lord's Supper (1 Cor.11: 23-32). It is good to remind ourselves that the word *discipline* is from the same Latin word from which the word *disciple* was derived. It's through teaching that we become a follower of Jesus.

When this ministry does lead to repentance, there is great joy among the membership and reason for celebration. When repentance doesn't happen, the elders will continue their ministry and at a certain point agree to ask the congregation to pray for this member, first without mentioning a name and then, if there is no change, with the name of the erring member. When ongoing ministry still does not lead to resolution, the elders will proceed with actual termination of membership. The congregation will then be notified of this with the urgent request to continue to pray for restoration (Matt. 18:17; 1 Cor. 5:1-5).

Even after excommunication, the elders and members continue in prayer and will reach out to the member. Those who have known the forgiveness of their own sins through the grace of Christ have great hope for all those who have not been able to accept that. They realize that it is by the power of the Holy Spirit that believers have been rescued from death to abundant life!

Bibliography

Books

Church Order and Rules for Synodical Procedure. Grand Rapids; MI: Christian Reformed Church in North America, 2003.

Engelhard, David H., and Leonard J. Hofman. *Manual of Christian Reformed Church Government, Revised Edition.* Grand Rapids, MI: Christian Reformed Church in North America, 2001.

Glynn, Gatrick. *God, the Evidence.* Rocklin, CA: Forum, 1997.

Hadaway, C. Kirk. *What Can We Do About Church Drop-outs?* Nashville: Abingdon Press, l990.

Haugk, Kenneth. *Twelve Keys to Effective Ministry to Inactive Members.* St. Louis, MO: Tebunan Ministries, 1997.

Hoge, Dean R. *Vanishing Boundaries: The Religion of Mainline Protestant Baby Boomers.* Louisville, KY: Westminster/John Knox Press, 1994.

____. *Why Catholics Drop Out.* Louisville, KY: Westminster/John Knox Press, 1997.

Lewis, C. S. *Mere Christianity.* New York: Touchstone, 1996.

Mittelberg, Mark. *Building Contagious Churches.* Grand Rapids, MI: Zondervan Publishing House, 2000.

Mulder, Karen, and Ginger Jurries. *The Compassionate Congregation: A Handbook for People Who Care.* Grand Rapids, MI: Faith Alive Christian Resources, 2002.

Plantinga Alvin. *Warranted Christian Belief.* New York: Oxford University Press, 2000.

Savage John S. *The Apathetic and Boring Church: Psychological and Theological Implications.* Pittsburg, NJ: Lead Consultants of America, l976.

Steinke, Peter L. *Healthy Congregations: A Systems Approach.* New York: Alban Institute, 1996.

____. *How Your Church Family Works: Understanding Congregations as Emotional Systems.* New York: Alban Institute, 1993.

Stott, John R. W. *Basic Christian Leadership.* Downers Grove, IL: InterVarsity Press, 2002.

Tamminga, Louis M. *Guiding God's People Through Changing Times: A Handbook for Elders.* Grand Rapids, MI: CRC Publications, 1997.

Van Groningen, Jay. *Changing Times/New Approaches: A Handbook for Deacons.* Grand Rapids, MI: CRC Publications/CRWRC, 1996.

Wagner, E. Glenn, with Steve Halliday. *Escape from the Church, Inc.: The Return of the Pastor-Shepherd.* Grand Rapids, MI: Zondervan Publishing House, 1999.

Willimon, William H. *Worship as Pastoral Care.* Nashville: Abingdon Press, l979.

Yancey, Philip. *Soul Survivor: How My Faith Survived the Church.* New York: Doubleday, 2001.

Yearbook. Grand Rapids, MI: Christian Reformed Church in North America, 2003.

____. *Reaching for the Invisible God: What Can We Expect to Find?* Grand Rapids, MI: Zondervan Publishing House, 2000.

Published Research Projects

Bouma, Gary D. "Keeping the Faithful: Patterns of Membership Retention in the Christian Reformed Church," *Sociological Analysis,* vol. 41, no. 3 (Fall 1980), pp. 259-264.

Beukema, John. "Today's Nesting Habits: Why Some Birds Have More Than One Church," *Leadership,* vol. 20 (Fall 1999), pp. 97-99.

Bullock, Robert. "God's Wandering Sheep," *Austin Seminary Bulletin: Faculty Edition,* vol. 86 (April 1971), pp. 44-45.

Commission on Children at Risk. "Hardwired to Connect: The New Scientific Case for Authoritative Communities," *A Report to the Nation.* New York: Institute for American Values, 2003.

Gregory, Stephen. "Without a Word: What Do You Do When People Leave Your Church Unannounced?" *Leadership,* vol. 18 (Winter 1997), pp. 91-93.

McIntosh, Ian Findlay. "Church Drop-outs," *Austin Seminary Bulletin: Faculty Edition,* vol. 86 (April 1971), pp. 5-43.

Musick, Mark A., and John Wilson. "Religious Switching for Marriage Reasons," *Sociology of Religion,* vol. 56 (Fall 1995), pp. 257-270.

The Unchurched American: Ten Years Later, Princeton, NJ: Princeton Research Center, 1988.